RISK & OTHER FOUR-LETTER WORDS

RISK & OTHER FOUR-LETTER WORDS

WALTER B. WRISTON

Harper & Row, Publishers, New York
Cambridge, Philadelphia, San Francisco, Washington
London, Mexico City, São Paulo, Singapore, Sydney

For Kathy
and
Dick, Cassy and Christopher

Portions of this work originally appeared in *Harvard Business Review* and *Economic Impact*.

A hardcover edition of this book is published by Harper & Row, Publishers, Inc.

First PERENNIAL LIBRARY edition published 1987.

Library of Congress Cataloging-in-Publication Data

Wriston, Walter B.
  Risk and other four letter words.

  "Perennial Library."
    1. Money—Addresses, essays, lectures.   2. Banks
and banking—Addresses, essays, lectures.
3. International economic relations—Addresses, essays,
lectures.   I. Title.
HG221.W937   1987   332.1   85-45245
ISBN 0-06-091389-4 (pbk.)

87 88 89 90 91 MPC 10 9 8 7 6 5 4 3 2 1

Contents

. ■ .

OBSERVATIONS FROM THE GLOBAL ATTIC

Foreword

▪ ■ ▪

Thornton Wilder wrote: "Every good thing in the world stands on the razor-edge of danger." He was right. The clear lesson of history is that individual liberty, the basic underpinning of American society, requires constant defense against the encroachment of the state. Ever since the Nobel laureate F. A. Hayek linked free markets with free men and women, the case for relieving the economy from overregulation assumed even deeper significance. A free society, if it is to remain free, requires citizens who take the risk of standing up to be counted on the issues of the day.

Over the last seventeen or eighteen years, the world produced one crisis after another, each one of which created a public controversy as to how it might be resolved. Some problems affected the region in which I live, some the emerging structure of a global financial market, and some the political alignments in the world. As these shocks rippled through our society, quite often the initial reaction was a spate of stories in print or on television suggesting that much of what we have built over the last two thousand years was about to be lost. It was not unusual to have these pronouncements accompanied by the observation that any solutions which were offered appeared to be "risky," with the word "risky" delivered in hushed tones. Even well-known business magazines are replete with headlines suggesting that Company X's strategy is "risky," or in a larger context a commentator may condemn the President's foreign policy since it entails "risks." In each of these articulations, the word "risk" is used as a pejorative, just as if there were alternatives in life that do not carry a greater or lesser degree of danger.

Americans in all walks of life steadily ignore the safety-first signs of society. In 1984, seven major candidates vied for the Democratic nomination for president, risking everything for the chance to run against one of the most popular presidents in history. I have no doubt there are dozens more even now planning and dreaming of winning the most difficult and demanding job in the world. What is true in politics obtains also in business. My banking experience was full of the excitement of meeting entrepreneurs with an idea they felt would create jobs and values, although more often than not mature corporate bureaucrats viewed them with alarm. A trucker named Malcom McLean once came to me with the idea of transporting by ship truck-trailers filled with cargo, and against all seagoing conventional wisdom built a great company called Sea-Land. More than that, he changed the very concept of moving freight. The ship became almost incidental to the fact the freight was picked up at someone's loading dock in one city or continent and delivered to someone else's receiving area. One of America's most respected shipping magnates paid a call on my boss to remind him that the proper way to take freight off ships was with a crane and cargo slings and expressed the hope that we would not find McLean's idea credit-worthy.

Today, the data show that 70 to 80 percent of all new jobs created in America in the last ten years were created by small start-up firms of less than 100 people. Some business persons knew an opportunity when they saw it and took the risk to make their dreams come true. While some don't make it in a competitive marketplace, many do. The free market in commerce, like a free political system, requires prudent risk-takers, men and women who know that risk is not synonymous with recklessness, but who also know that there is no real security in this life. Apparently, however, many commentators still do not remember Gilbert Chesterton's remarks that "democracy is a dangerous trade."

The essays that constitute this volume are edited versions of speeches that I wrote and delivered, often at the height of some public controversy. Today it is hard to recall the intensity of the feelings created during particular crises. There is always the temptation to revise the conclusions reached in the midst of the battle in order to bring them into harmony with what has been revealed in the blinding clarity of hindsight. This temptation has been resisted, and the judgments made at the time will have to stand on their own.

It has been my belief that it takes about ten years from the time an idea is launched on a college campus, or in some other forum, until the Congress of the United States passes a law reflecting some version of the concept. That is as it should be, but it is also true that if there are competing ideas in the marketplace, better decisions will result. The Salvation Army was founded by an extraordinary person who asked the question, "Why should the devil have all the good songs?" These essays were written following a similar theory. Why should the advocates of bigger government and more regulation, which lead inevitably to the loss of individual liberty, be so lightly opposed in the battle of ideas? During much of the period during which these speeches were written, the proponents of freer markets, with some notable exceptions, were not much in evidence. This was particularly true in the financial service industry. Some businessmen even called for price and wage controls, or legislation to protect or preserve an entrenched market position. Since the written and spoken word clearly can and does have a role in shaping the political process, I like to think that America's return toward a freer economic system got a small nudge along the way from some of the contributions to the debate contained in this volume.

THE INDIVIDUAL AND SOCIETY

· ■ ·

Not Every Battle
Is Armageddon

· ■ ·

E ach of the various cultures of the world has something to
teach us; one can, for instance, borrow from part of the
philosophy of Buddha and project it against our contemporary
environment. Buddha said, in effect: "Don't just do something, stand there." This reversal of the usual American advice
has a certain relevancy for today.

All of us are flooded daily with messages on radio, television, and in the newspapers, which, if taken at face value,
would leave the human race no alternative but to prepare for
mass self-destruction. The communicators of the world pound
home the message day after day that every problem has become critical: Every battle is Armageddon.

Without in any way downgrading the problems of our
time, I suggest that the people who tell you the world is about
to stop, and repeat it constantly, are guilty of a kind of intellectual overkill. They have either never read any history, or, if
they have, failed to understand it.

A columnist, writing in the *New York Times,* once made a
dire prognostication about our country when the Senate
passed a minor piece of legislation that in the end came to
nothing and by now has been forgotten: "Poor old Union! Its

great and generous dreams falling one by one to dusty death."
He was a modern reincarnation of the British scholar Lord
Bryce, who studied our Constitution at the time of its birth and
solemnly averred that it was all sail and no anchor and that the
ship of state would founder.

His verdict was not proclaimed electronically around the
world. In fact, it passed almost unnoticed. There was no
clamor for a new Constitutional Convention to remedy our
disastrous mistake, so clearly identified by an "expert."

Today, however, we all live in Marshall McLuhan's "global village" and Chicken Little runs through our living rooms
on every hourly newscast. The process gives a new dimension
to the word "synergy."

Barbara Tuchman, one of our distinguished historians, has
observed that "the fact of being reported multiplies the apparent extent of any deplorable development by five-to-ten fold."

A study of how people learned of the shooting of President
John Kennedy in 1963 showed that 44 percent of the people
knew it within fifteen minutes, 62 percent within forty-five
minutes, and 90 percent within an hour. About half of the
people heard about the event from radio and television and
they notified the rest either in person or by telephone. It was
the first time in history that the population of an entire continent learned about a single event in an hour's time. And that
was twenty years ago!

Today, cameras zoom in on the face of the man struck by
the rock or the policeman's club. Armies that clashed by
night now appear in our living rooms. I do not in any way
argue that this is bad; far from it. But I have to observe that
for the first time in the history of Man, our society, with all
the flaws inherent in human nature, all the breakdowns in
technology, and all of our social foibles, is communicated
instantly to the world. Things will inevitably go wrong, because men still are not gods. But because all the failures, the
mistakes, and the accidents intrude upon our consciousness
in an almost unbroken stream, our fear of the future increases exponentially.

The fact that the world has had the technology to destroy this planet for more than thirty years, but has not done so, is noteworthy but not newsworthy. Nevertheless, it is critical to all else. It represents what Barbara Tuchman calls "the persistence of the normal." And it is this persistence that gets us past the crisis.

If we kept a running inventory of trouble in today's world, reasonable people might conclude that the world was about ready to collapse. All the elements of disaster are present. And yet somehow the world still functions—despite a full-scale war between Iran and Iraq which has consumed several hundred thousand lives, a Soviet invasion and war of attrition in Afghanistan, a complex and dangerous factional war in Lebanon, the military adventures of Libya in Africa, the presence of Cuban troops in Angola, the wars in Central America, the fight for the Falkland Islands, the war in Cambodia, and struggles in other parts of the arc of Asia.

This is not to say that there are not always present real dangers of great magnitude which require our best efforts to manage—there are. Indeed, one seems to succeed another with great rapidity. What is underestimated is the ability of mankind—using that term in its broadest sense—to act and react and to survive.

Those who say that Armageddon is here and that the world will stop tomorrow completely miss the main message of life. The real news in American society is not that our problems are complex and have multiplied, but rather that our sensitivity to these problems is greater now than at any time in the long history of man. This is enormous progress in your lifetime and mine, for every problem-solver knows that quantifying the problem, and recognizing it for what it is, is often half the battle. One grows weary of strident voices whose owners' ignorance of the past is matched only by the extravagance of their language. Our generation, like each one before it, has made mistakes, but at least we are facing the major problems of our time with candor and energy. Our record is not that bad. I agree with the late historian at the University of Montana Mr. K. Ross Toole, who said that he was "tired of the tyranny of spoiled brats." He wrote:

> My generation has made America the most affluent country on earth. It has tackled, head-on, a racial problem, which no nation on earth in the history of mankind had dared to do. It has publicly declared war on poverty and it has gone to the moon; it has desegregated schools and abolished polio; it has presided over the beginning of what is probably the greatest social and economic revolution in man's history. It has begun these things, not finished them. It has declared itself, and committed itself, and taxed itself, and damn near run itself into the ground in the cause of social justice and reform.

That is not a message of despair, but of hope and achievement. It is a record of sensitivity to our environment of a magnitude never before achieved.

The Bible, for example, tells us that "the poor are always with us." The fact that our generation does not accept this as a God-given state of affairs, but rather is putting its energy and its skill and its imagination to work to reverse this ancient state, is good news, not bad. That we Americans have not achieved in a few years what the world has been unable to do in two thousand years is not a valid cause for despair. To the contrary, it is a cause for optimism.

We are similarly sensitive to our environment, and the need for us all to do something to improve its quality, not only because we are anchored in our communities and will continue to be, but also because we now have a deeper interest in the condition of our environment. This state of affairs is both a circumstance and a subject that would not even have been thought of twenty years ago. The fact that we have all become acutely aware of our mistreatment of our environment is, again, not a cause for despair, but rather, in any kind of perspective, a source of encouragement. We have now defined the problem, which went largely undetected for a long time. We overlooked it because it was growing at such a rate that only yesterday no crisis was foreseen. Half of the people in our nation have been born since the end of World War II. It is perfectly plain that twice the number of people living on the same land mass would cause a pollution problem even if we had been much more skillful than we had been.

After all, what did Adam and Eve do with the apple core? Pollution is caused by people and it starts with the throwing of a beer can out the window of a student's car while he is on the way to an environmental demonstration.

Before the poor old Union goes down to dusty death, it would be useful to remember that the Greek civilization, which many admire so much, was in fact built upon human slavery. It might be instructive also to recall that George Washington was a slave owner, and that in those days most people of his time, who suffered a long and costly war for liberty, did not make a distinction between owning slaves and supporting the Declaration of Independence. That great document was silent on this subject.

In this day of concern about voter registration, literacy tests, and raising the legal drinking age, we overlooked the fact that the principal drafter of the Declaration of Independence, Thomas Jefferson, believed that only a man who held real property should be entitled to the vote. Far from going down to dusty death, the American dream steadily has sharpened its focus; but the clamor for instant solutions to ancient problems obscures the enormous progress that we have made.

Consequently, anyone in our society whose eyesight and hearing are not totally impaired is likely to believe that we are on a collision course with doomsday. Considering the amount of time and space devoted to predictions of impending disaster, it would appear that we have sought to validate a variation on Gresham's law: Bad news drives out good.

Our compulsion to turn every scrap of bad news into a full-blown crisis distorts our perspective. It neglects to remind us that troubles may be news, but they are by no means new.

This negative emphasis ignores the decisive role of human ingenuity in a free society, which invariably produces a coping mechanism.

Alarmists' curves frequently are based upon downward trends. As early as the sixth chapter of Genesis, some believed the world was headed downhill. The doomsayers were already looking back upon better times: "There were giants in the earth in those days."

Prophets of doom fail to appreciate man's inherent ability to adjust and innovate. The British economist Thomas Malthus predicted in 1798 that the imbalance between population growth and food production would cause the world to starve to death. The doomsayers called it Malthus's Iron Law. As time has proved, it was neither iron nor law. Like many of our current crop of transient experts, Malthus fell into the oldest trap of all in the prognostication game. He underestimated everyone's intelligence but his own; he was incapable of imagining that out of the Industrial Revolution would come reapers, threshers, combines, and tractors. He did not foresee that quantum jump in productivity. Nor did he envision agricultural improvements creating such abundance that foolish governments would pay farmers not to cultivate the soil.

A third fault accounts for the inability of the doomsayers accurately to predict what will happen. They cling to the belief that there are accepted absolutes in a world of rapidly changing value systems. As the French poet Paul Valéry put it: "We often tend to be marching backward into the future."

Examples abound. A presidential commission appointed by Herbert Hoover in 1929 later reported to Franklin D. Roosevelt on how to plot our course through 1952. The report was in thirteen volumes, prepared by five hundred researchers. The summary alone filled sixteen hundred pages. Yet there was not a word about atomic energy, jet propulsion, antibiotics, transistors, or many other significant developments that occurred by 1952. The World's Fair of 1939, which was dedicated to the World of Tomorrow, not only failed to suggest any of these advances, but did not even entertain the idea of space travel. The late Herman Kahn's opus on the year 2000 never mentioned pollution, nor was there any real emphasis on the energy shortage. The people who have come closest to predicting the future are some of the science fiction writers, unencumbered by elaborate research or prestigious committees, but with the courage to dream. Jules Verne's wild imagination proved to be more prophetic than the calculations of Malthus.

Our latter-day Malthusians, whose forecasts are often dignified with computer printouts—which substitute for the ancients' ox entrails in modern-day occult prediction—appear oblivious of the fact that man, given the proper incentive and freedom to act, has repeatedly found substitutes for dwindling materials. The United States was denied 90 percent of its sources of natural rubber during World War II, but technological ingenuity created synthetic rubber, which is now more widely and flexibly used than the natural product. One of the most common substances in the world is bauxite, but it was not regarded as much of an asset until the way to manufacture aluminum was perfected. Coal was not even considered a resource before the steam age, nor was uranium highly valued before the atomic age. Since the Industrial Revolution, resources have grown exponentially, step by step, with man's ability to apply fresh technology to his needs. These experiences of yesterday are relevant today. I do not assert that history repeats itself, but offer a reminder that the human story did not begin with today's crisis.

This propensity of Americans to overstate and overkill is not new. The only difference today is that the technical scope and reach of our communications are much wider that ever before in history. One man saying that everything is wrong can command coast-to-coast attention in living color, a power not given to an absolute monarch a century ago.

One of the great optimists of America was Walt Whitman, who usually sang of the joys and promises of our land. In 1870, however, he wrote: "Never was there, perhaps, more hollowness of heart than at present. Genuine belief seems to have left us. . . . We live in an atmosphere of hypocrisy throughout. . . . The depravity of the business classes of the country is not less than has been supposed, but infinitely greater. The official services of America . . . are saturated in corruption, bribery, falsehood, maladministration." These views, published in a pamphlet, attracted limited attention in those days, and despite Whitman's name and fame, only a tiny fraction of the population was even aware of his momentary despair.

Whitman, fortunately, reminded us, on another occasion, of a more important, universal truth. That is that these institutions, which are said to be in trouble, are made up of people like you and me. The American system has been built not upon the worship of institutions but upon a belief in the worth of the individual.

Whitman put it this way:

> O I see flashing that this America is only you and me,
> Its power, weapons, testimony, are you and me,
> Its crimes, lies, thefts, defections, are you and me,
> Its Congress is you and me, the officers, capitols, armies,
>   ships, are you and me.

Whitman did not say that America was a collection of groups or institutions. He said it was you and me. We do not educate groups; we educate individuals. Part of our education must be that each of us has an obligation to pass on to our children our hard-won individual liberty, which must be reasserted if our freedom is to endure.

One reason for the deep pessimism of our generation's communicators is that somehow they got it into their minds that prior to yesterday America was largely a happy and serene country. They brush under the rug the violent upsets of 1919 and 1920, years when wholesale violations of our civil liberties were carried out.

They apparently forget the Whiskey Rebellion, when Appalachian farmers protested against Alexander Hamilton's formula for debt and tax collection. They overlook the urban riots between newly arrived immigrants and so-called native Americans, which took place in the mid-1800s. Somehow the racial and labor disturbances throughout the late 1930s have faded in their memories, if indeed they ever knew about them.

It is interesting to speculate about what some of the noisy undertakers of American democracy would say if they took the time to read our country's history and stumbled across the Espionage and Sedition Acts of 1917 and 1918. These two bills provided a ten-thousand-dollar fine and a twenty-year prison sentence for such felonies as interfering with the draft, encouraging disloyalty, obstructing the sale of United States Treasury Bonds or using "disloyal or abusive language" about the government, the Constitution, the flag, or the uniform. Some two thousand seven hundred people were convicted of violating it, including a man who ran for President and polled more than one million votes. Quite naturally, these statutes were tested in the courts, and their constitutionality was *upheld* by the Supreme Court.

During the height of the so-called Red Scare in 1919, a duly constituted jury in Hammond, Indiana, took less than five minutes to acquit the assassin of an alien who yelled "to hell with the United States." Early the following year, a salesman in a clothing store in Connecticut was sentenced to six months in jail for remarking to a customer that Lenin was one of the brainiest of the world's political leaders. When the Attorney General made a public statement that the work of private counterespionage and vigilante groups was unnecessary and unwanted, the *New York Times* complained that the Attorney General "has perhaps been a little hasty in telling the patriotic and defensive societies that their help in guarding the Republic is neither needed nor welcomed."

An imperfect past does not excuse an imperfect present, but a knowledge of past realities and past mistakes is critical if we are to avoid the same mistakes twice.

Saul Bellow, the novelist, made this point when he wrote: "Maybe civilization is coming to an end, but it still exists, and meanwhile we have our choice: We can either rain more blows on it, or try to redeem it."

It is my view that we Americans are trying with some success to redeem it. We have not solved all of our problems, but we have faced them squarely. We sometimes are assaulted so much by our failures that we overlook the progress that has been made. We hear too much of what John Gardner has called "the currently fashionable mixture of passion and incompetence." Against that background, we might consider the advice of an eminent American historian who, from the vantage point of eighty years, wrote: "Extravagance in the interpretation of current events destroys perspective and contributes nothing to poise and stability. It plays into the hands of the extremists at both ends of the political spectrum."

Therefore, the one remaining event capable of taking everyone by surprise would be a continuous period of, say, three weeks in midsummer *without* the discovery and breathless proclamation of a single new crisis. I predict that the ripple effect of such a startling nonevent would quickly circle the globe and produce record levels of consternation.

Sunday rotogravure editors would rummage in old police records for unsolved ax murders, and financial commentators would be reduced to foraging in their files for old economic crises to refurbish. Program chairpersons for countless fraternal and professional organizations, having no crisis topic for luncheon speakers, would revert to photo-slide lectures on family excursions to Yellowstone National Park—exchanging one "Old Faithful" for another. Business economists would interrupt their internal dispute over whether it is an art or a science they practice, long enough to issue a reassuring joint communiqué stating that the absence of an immediate economic crisis is not serious—but merely a temporary aberration that will correct itself as soon as some fine tuning is done with fiscal and monetary policies. Congressional leaders would further assure us that if no better crisis occurs spontaneously within thirty days, they will manufacture one.

Though I can stand the absence of crisis as well as anyone,

I earnestly hope there will be no interruption in the steady flow of entirely manageable crises that we have survived in recent years—though some lowering of the decibel level would be helpful.

Perhaps then we could restore our perspective and rejoice about our sensitivity to human problems—which is, in fact, unmatched in the history of this or any other country.

Nothing that is good comes easily, so it is impossible to render a pat formula for solving the world's problems. But I recall an inscription on the wall of one of the congressional hearing rooms in Washington. It says:

> Due to the shortage of experienced trumpet players, doomsday will be postponed for three weeks.

So really Armageddon never arrives, and people with their intellectual capital invested in the end of the world are not getting a good return.

The Great American Transference Machine

■ ■ ■

Every village square used to have a statue of some national hero, and there are many still standing. Sometimes they were cast in the likeness of a departed political leader or sometimes a military hero. One of the statues that I have always liked best represents neither a statesman nor a general, nor even an ordinary soldier in some past war. It stands atop the State House in Providence, Rhode Island. Contrary to expectations, it is not a likeness of Roger Williams, George Washington, or some other colonial patriot. It is a statue identified only as "The Independent Man," and he was put there to watch over the affairs taking place under the dome of the State House.

I like to think that if we look hard enough, we might see the Independent Man waving at us, trying to redirect our attention to something we seem to have forgotten. I think he would like to remind us that the people of little Rhode Island put him atop the State House because they understood the importance of the individual in a democratic society and because they knew that a government of and by the people can be no better than the citizens themselves.

The importance of the Independent Man in our society has

been obscured by a constant stream of data about our individual helplessness in the face of big government, big business, big institutions, and big media. This theme of individual helplessness is viewed as a modern phenomenon by people who apparently do not realize that only in very recent history has the grip of feudalism been broken. Throughout most of the tenure of the human race on this planet, a feeling of individual helplessness has been the rule, not the exception. The miracle of modern communication not only keeps us painfully aware that we face problems in our society, but also suggests that those problems must be different in degree and in kind from those addressed by our forefathers.

There is little doubt that our days are troubled, that the world is large and complex, but this condition is not new. We are told in graphic terms about the specter of nuclear extinction, but few journalists remember and none write of the time in the fourteenth century when the Black Death killed at least one-third, and perhaps as much as one-half, of the population of Europe and Asia. No one had any idea how to halt its deadly spread, or any reason to believe that the human race would survive. Tens of thousands of European villages disappeared from the face of the earth and several centuries passed before Europe's population was restored. Barbara Tuchman recounts that "the sense of a vanishing future created a kind of dementia of despair . . . people felt in Walsingham's words that 'the world could never again regain its former prosperity.' " These words have the contemporary ring of the seven o'clock news.

The study of history has its uses, and one of them is to provide some measure of perspective, so lacking in our world today. But even those who cannot, or will not, learn from history might still profit from a more careful reading of the daily papers. All this nonsense about the powerlessness of the individual came at a point in history when we witnessed one man, Lech Walesa of Poland, take on the enormous might of the Soviet Union.

It was a stunning achievement of enormous import. No

matter that Walesa was eventually jailed. He demonstrated that even a repressive government must have the support of its people. In our own country we elected new leaders who challenged not only an incumbent government but the perceived political and economic wisdom of the previous four decades.

As we look around and take stock, we can perceive that even when the problems we face may be significantly different from those of yesterday, their solution still depends upon individuals working the problem and not upon vague programs constructed by institutions. And yet, almost imperceptibly, we have been shifting not only the responsibility for a solution to someone else but the blame for the problem itself. All of our troubles, we are told, are caused by the government or by institutions which are somehow separate and apart from you and me and which, therefore, have the responsibility to resolve them. John Stuart Mill never suffered from this illusion.

> If we ask ourselves on what causes and conditions good
> government in all its senses . . . depends, we find . . .
> the one which transcends all others is the qualities of
> the human beings comprising the society over which
> government is exercised.

What have we been doing to these qualities of human beings—in short, to our individual value systems? It takes more than a little study to find out, because our attention has been directed away from the real problem. This is not unusual, because one of the fundamentals of stage show magic, demagogic politics, and good football is misdirection. With attention focused on one hand, the other is left free to do its work unseen; or while most of the players flow to the right side, the ball carrier is running to the left. In magic and in sports, one has to sustain the illusion for only a moment to pull off the trick or the play. In politics and economics the time frame required to succeed with misdirection is longer, but by the time it is exposed, the clock may have run out for the nation.

The art of misdirection may also be applied to oneself. One does not have to look far to learn that an individual's moral behavior is increasingly proclaimed to be nobody else's business. We impose fewer and fewer restrictions on our own conduct as individuals, asserting everyone's right to a personal life style. Yet simultaneously we impose harsher, and increasingly irrational, restrictions on all of our institutions. We seem to feel that if we demand less of ourselves, the balance can be maintained by requiring more of corporate and government entities—a sort of moral equivalent to the law of thermodynamics. The results are reflected in endless paradoxes. Irving Kristol has pointed out that it is now perfectly legal for a nineteen-year-old girl to perform in a pornographic movie, but only if she is paid the minimum wage.

People's right to live as they please has been accompanied by the growing conviction that there are no honest men and women left in the world. Since no one can be required by law to have principles, we conclude that no one does. Acting on that assumption, Congress passed the Ethics in Government Act, which requires a listing of the income from every source and any conflict of interest, real or imagined, now or in the future. The only office in the United States Government that now can be filled from a profession schooled in that discipline without attracting comments about conflicts of interest is that of the Attorney General—perhaps because lawyers write the conflict-of-interest laws and only lawyers become attorneys general. No one who knows as much about energy as the Attorney General is supposed to know about law would be allowed to run the Department of Energy—a critical problem of our time. All this is done in the name of trying to assure ourselves that our institutions will display standards of morality higher than those we set for ourselves.

Looking at recent history, I think that we came close to our political nadir a few years ago in the Senate confirmation hearings of Nelson Rockefeller as Vice-President of the

United States. Whether or not one admires his record is immaterial. Here was a man who, in his words, "never wanted to be vice-president of anything," but agreed to step into the breach at a time when we were rapidly approaching a grave constitutional crisis. No one in the Senate seemed interested that the man had repeatedly been elected to high office by the people of his own state, or that he had served many Presidents of both parties over several decades. Instead, the hearings turned into a financial peep show—a media event that almost totally ignored the national crisis which was the cause of the hearings. Can anyone really believe that those who conducted the protracted hearings were motivated by the fear that something might still lie hidden in Nelson Rockefeller's highly public past that should disqualify him for high office? The fact that he was confirmed, and served with distinction, does not excuse the excesses of those hearings any more than the fact that real Communists do exist could excuse the witch hunts of Senator Joe McCarthy.

Most of the people present at our Constitutional Convention were landed, educated men with personal perspectives and problems. yet they forged a document that balanced the power between various sections of the country and the society in a way that stood the test of time. Had they been obliged to pass the conflict-of-interest test, it is doubtful that many of them could have walked through the door.

Perhaps it is time to examine this phenomenon; not the law so much as the philosophy which created it. A great teacher once told me that every time you read a new book, you should also go back and read an old one. It is not a bad prescription if we want to regain some perspective. There are many old books that deserve an occasional visit. One was written by a man named Smith who saw the world clearly and had few illusions about human nature. He understood the relationship between the individual and society. Adam Smith, like John Stuart Mill, knew that society and the individuals who make it up are one and the same thing. Smith believed in a strong national defense which depends on government. But he also argued that a strong defense is impossible without a strong economy and that the strength of the economy in turn depends on individual effort. Smith's emphasis on the individual is relevant not only to economics but also to education, which is an individual experience. There is no such thing as an institutional education, because buildings do not learn. No one has ever heard of state morality, or state freedom. Like the intellectual virtues, these are the exclusive province of the individual. No one ever educated a state or an institution. Only individuals learn. The great American transference machine has attempted to switch to institutions traits that only individuals can possess, like morality and honesty. At the same time, it has set up a clatter which suggests that there are no honest men and women, only clean institutions. This is an intellectual cul-de-sac. When virtue leaves the individual, it has no place to go. I think it is time to say so with clarity and vigor. The case was put succinctly by Edward Norman:

> The moral authority of the individual, which in the past sustained freedom, is being sapped by the growing moralism of the advocates of collectivism . . . we need to be more aware than we are that freedom has no built-in presumptives of its own.

If you would look to another old book written by a man who understood much about America, the words of de Tocqueville come to mind:

> It would seem as if the rulers of our time sought only to use men in order to make things great. I wish that they would try a little more to make a great man; that would set less value on the work and more upon the workman.

The town of Appleton, Wisconsin, when I was a boy growing up there, had a police force, a school system, a mayor, and a jail—and they were all busy. We did not think of individuals who broke the law or ignored the mores of the time as a reflection on the town. They were a reflection on no one but themselves. We did not speak of Appleton's morality or intone about the ethics of the town. Even today we have not transferred individual traits to towns to quite the same extent that we have to some governments and private institutions, perhaps because the absurdity is just too obvious. This was what Edmund Burke had in mind at the time of our American Revolution when he said: "I do not know the method of drawing up an indictment against a whole people."

Yet the transference machine operates today across the whole spectrum of society, from explanations of why Johnny can't read to the high cost of health care. A recent foundation study came to the remarkable conclusion that good individual teachers have a marked effect on how much students learn. If the report were not so solemn it would be hilarious. No one denies the enormous cost of health care in America, which now amounts to over 10 percent of our gross national product. What we do not want to come to grips with is the enormous cost of self-inflicted disease which inflates hospital costs. The leading cause of admission in many hospitals is alcoholism. The link between cigarette smoking and several diseases is too close to be ignored. Whether we eat too much, smoke too much, or drink too much is an individual choice and is not controlled by big government, or big institutions, or big media, or caused by the system. Yet somehow it is always "the country" which has a drinking problem, or an obesity problem, or a health problem, and only the government ought to be doing something about it.

There is still time in America to respond to that independent man who cries to us from a rooftop in Rhode Island. We should be wary of any group which asserts that it alone has discovered what social morality ought to be, no less than we should guard against any group that would combine political and economic power enforced by the rule of law. We must take great care to avoid rendering unto Caesar the things that are not his, for the long history of man shows that when you do, Caesar ends up with everything. The independent man is not waving at the *system*. He is beckoning to you and me to choose, to play our part. He is calling to us to participate in a process, to go where no government can lead us.

The Other
Nine Amendments

· ■ ·

Sometimes, in our day-to-day concerns with mundane problems, we fail to perceive accurately the changing nature of the world around us. It is a common failing, often with unsettling consequences, and all should take counsel from an incident recorded by Jean de Joinville, the French chronicler of the Crusades. He relates, in his semihistorical account, how a young crusader named Acephalous reached up and thoughtfully stroked his beard after being beheaded by a sword-swinging Saracen soldier. Those who fail to remember that freedom is indivisible may end up emulating Acephalous.

One of the reasons intellectual freedom has survived all these years is not only that it is an older concept than market freedom, but also because the faculties of thousands of colleges and universities are articulate defenders of their cause. It is a popular cause, as well it should be. The intellectual community, however, doesn't act much differently than any other sector of society when it comes under attack. When the late Senator McCarthy was at the height of his vituperative powers and seeing a Communist on every campus, there were depressingly few academics, such as Nathan Pusey, who stood up to do battle with him. In the end it was a tough lawyer from

Boston who finally brought McCarthy down. The lawyer had the silent cheers but not much articulate support from the academic community, many of whom feared retribution from the senator's acidic tongue.

The business person has had no such guild to defend his right to free speech and free enterprise. Unlike the intellectual community, the businesspeople of the world perceive themselves to be always under the threat of retaliation. Whether rightly or wrongly, they expect this retaliation to be aided and abetted by those who do not trust the free markets in goods even while they promote free markets in ideas. A railroad executive who publicly attacked the corrosive bureaucracy of the Interstate Commerce Commission, which was largely responsible for regulating our railroads into bankruptcy, feared that his next plea for a rate increase would be prejudged. A merchandiser who dares challenge some arbitrary rule promulgated by the Federal Trade Commission fears that bureaucracy will live to fight him another day. A banker who suggests that the regulatory attitudes on interstate banking are anticonsumer fears that retribution will be visited upon him by the authorities in Washington.

Many ardent defenders of freedom of speech argue that advertising copy for products and services is a fit subject for government regulation, lest the dumb citizen be bilked of his money by buying an inferior product. If inferior, doubtful, or even false opinions and ideas are put between the covers of a book, published in the newspapers, or flashed on television, the citizen no longer needs the protection of government regulation. It is an interesting piece of intellectual hairsplitting, based in part on our view of our own importance.

One thing that keeps us all going is that we view our means of earning our daily bread as making an important contribution to our world. Without bankers the economy would not function. Without bakers the world would starve. Without teachers there would be ignorance. Without politicians there would be anarchy. Make the list as long as you like and fill in the blanks with any known occupation. Raymond Aron, the late French political thinker, put it in this way:

> A superficial explanation for their preference for free speech among intellectuals runs in terms of vertical interests . . . intellectuals are engaged in the pursuit of truth, while others are merely engaged in earning a livelihood. One follows a profession, usually a learned one, while the other follows a trade or a business.

On the other side of the fence, some businessmen speak scornfully of intellectuals who have never met a payroll.

The fact that I argue for a free market in goods and services, and that such a market would benefit my company, does not make my argument unsound. Self-interest and public policy can coincide and often do. No one attacks a newsman demanding freedom of the press just because the pursuit of that objective is what puts money in his pocket and dinner on his table. No one attacks a professor arguing for academic freedom, although its absence might cause the scholar to lose his job.

It is anachronistic that many who champion everyone's right to dissent and to demonstrate, without any government restraint whatsoever, are often the most outspoken advocates of eliminating freedom in other sectors.

If the proponents of central planning came right out and said that they wanted to create an economic police state, their cause would never get off the ground. So they resort to "doublespeak," the usual camouflage for the ultimate use of force against the individual. The Austrian economist Ludwig von Mises summed it up when he wrote:

> All this talk, the state should do this or that, ultimately means the police should force consumers otherwise than they would behave spontaneously. In such proposals as let us raise farm prices, let us raise wage rates, let us lower profit . . . the *us* ultimately refers to the police.

Yet, the authors of these projects protest that they are planning for freedom and industrial democracy.

Perhaps the oldest lesson of history is that an assault on one aspect of freedom is an attack on the whole, as the framers of the Constitution were well aware. To think that the bell which tolls for economic freedom does not toll for academic freedom, or for freedom of the press, is a delusion, and a dangerous one. The vigilance of the press, which helped smoke out some of the misdeeds of Watergate, should be equally focused on the economic non sequiturs coming from some of Washington's prominent citizens.

Attacks on the system that has produced our relative affluence, as well as our freedom, come in part from people seeking power and in part from a failure to understand the American experience. Pulitzer Prize historian Daniel Boorstin put it this way:

> There is an increasing tendency . . . to blame the United States for lacking many of the ills which have characterized European history. Our lack of poverty is called materialism, our lack of political dogma is called aimlessness and confusion.

All proposals for a managed economy rest on an underestimation of the intelligence of the American people. They assume that you and I are just not smart enough to decide how to spend the money we earn. The decision must be made for us by a wise government. The intellectual arrogance of those who would substitute their judgment for that of the American people is amazing.

The clash between governmental economic planning and personal liberty is inevitable because, in the end, governmental allocation of either economic or intellectual resources requires the use of force. This power must be continuously increased to block opposition, to generate public acceptance, and to suppress doubts about the competence of the planner.

No plan that encompasses a continent with the infinite variety of America and containing thousands of parts can possibly be agreed to by experts let alone endorsed by a majority of the people. Even if by some miracle we could get all the fiscalists and monetarists to concur, the ultimate decisions would be much more political than economic. It would be impossible to get a majority vote in the Congress on every item in the economy that would have to be allocated, priced, and assigned priority. Since simultaneous political and economic agreement is a virtual impossibility, these decisions have to be delegated to the planner and, thus, can never represent the will of the majority. Such action, by definition, destroys the premise on which American democracy rests.

Those great principles of our government laid down by our Founding Fathers embody a vast distrust of centralized governmental power and an unswerving dedication to the proposition that government rests on the consent of the governed. Nevertheless, whenever we create the conditions that cause our system to appear to falter, whether through inflation or corruption, people who would destroy our liberty press forward with plans the founders rejected—old plans dressed in a new vocabulary. A good many years ago, John Randolph, the Virginia lawmaker, foresaw the danger and put it this way:

> The people of this country, if ever they lose their
> liberties, will do it by sacrificing some great principle of
> government to temporary passion.

As always, passions abound in our land. When the heat rises, our memory of fundamentals seems to fade. We forget that the traditional optimism of the American people is an absolute essential to a democracy. We hear, from time to time, a rising chorus attacking the beneficent American economic system.

People who should know better waffle about human freedom and, in the moment of passion that John Randolph feared, have even suggested that some form of dictatorship might not be so bad after all. In the 1930s, Senator David Reed of Pennsylvania voiced it bluntly: "If this country ever needed a Mussolini, it needs one now." The senator had obviously not read an article written in 1932 by a former Italian journalist, who stated with great clarity:

> The Fascist State has drawn into itself even the economic activities of the nation . . . its influence reaches every aspect of the national life . . . all the political, economic and spiritual forges of the nation.

The journalist's name was Mussolini, and he, you recall, went on to prove his point.

The admiration in the United States for the way Mussolini made the trains run on time was widespread. The *New York Times* in May 1933 reported that the atmosphere in Washington was "strangely reminiscent of Rome in the first weeks after the march of the Blackshirts, of Moscow at the beginning of the Five-Year Plan. . . . The new capital . . . presupposes just such a highly centralized, all-inclusive government as is now in the making." In the 1930s it began to look more and more as if we would sacrifice some great principle and lose our liberty.

The resident philosopher in Washington in those days was Rexford Guy Tugwell, who held in contempt the consumers' ability to choose and wanted large state-controlled corporations along Fascist lines. It was all very simple and logical. He put it this way: "When industry is government and government is industry, the dual conflict deepest in our modern institutions will be abated." This old idea was revived in the mid-1970s under the new name "benchmark" corporations. In 1984, George Orwell told us, the concept would be set to music in a telescreen jingle that went: "Under the spreading chestnut tree, I sold you and you sold me."

The first major step that this nation took toward merging government and industry, and toward the total abandonment of the free market system, was the enactment of the legislation that created the National Recovery Administration. The NRA, with its famous Blue Eagle symbol, soon began grinding out hundreds of "codes" repealing economic freedom and arbitrarily fixing wages, prices, and hours.

In the temporary passion of that moment, many businessmen welcomed the idea of controls and were openly pleased with the idea of an escape from competition. "Codes" in the 1930s were the equivalent of the modern euphemism "guidelines." Those codes ultimately affected some twenty-two million workers. As with all schemes that require people to behave in a way they would not choose of their own free will, force eventually had to be used against the populace. Since the NRA codes required citizens to make decisions that were contrary to their own economic interests, penalties for noncompliance were severe. Tailors were arrested, indicted, convicted, and sentenced because their prices for pressing a pair of pants were a nickel below the relevant NRA code. Farmers were fined for planting wheat that they ate on their own farms. Barbers who charged less than the code rate for a shave and a haircut were subject to fines of up to five hundred dollars. Even the village handyman was prosecuted, since he did not fit the multiple wage and hour scale set up by the codes.

The complexity of the codes soon antagonized labor as well as management. The average factory worker, who had been earning twenty-five dollars a week, was cut back to eighteen dollars and sixty cents under NRA codes. As a result, strikes became a way of life, and auto workers, frustrated by red tape, began calling the NRA the National Run Around. When the textile code authority cut production in the mills in 1934, another great strike began in the South. Before the strike ended, the national guard was called out in seven states and scores of textile workers were killed and wounded. A few months later, NRA administrator General Hugh Johnson resigned in a storm of criticism—or, as he phrased it, "an ever increasing volley of dead cats."

As was the case with the rights of minorities in the 1950s and '60s, or with Watergate in the '70s, few had the courage to challenge the power of the state. A fairly small business, the Schechter Poultry Company, refused the NRA standards of "fitness" regulating the slaughter of chickens. When the case reached the Supreme Court, the NRA was unanimously declared unconstitutional. The Court wrote: "Such a delegation of powers is unknown to our law and it is utterly inconsistent with the constitutional prerogatives and duties of Congress."

After the decision was read, Justice Louis Brandeis said to one of President Roosevelt's legal aides, "I want you to go back and tell the President that we're not going to let the government centralize everything." That was a call to return to fundamental American principles.

What I am suggesting is that we must examine with great care and skepticism any proposition that government regulation of goods and services is any more a legitimate function of government now than it was then. It is predicated on the dogma that consumers lack the intelligence to make choices, that they are incapable of sorting out a good idea from a bad one without government help. We should question the logic that leads some people to conclude that a so-called truth-in-advertising law is good, but a truth-in-media law is bad. On a purely logical basis, it is hard to sustain the argument that the public is unable intelligently to choose among competing dog foods without government help, but it is competent to sort the true meaning of a senator's speech.

More and more educators feel the hand of government within their campuses, despite our long tradition of academic freedom. Academicians are learning the old lesson that if you take the king's shilling, you will do the king's bidding. If you accept the proposition that government intervention in the dissemination of ideas is bad, which is one I strongly hold, you must then review in your own mind whether it makes any sense to argue for governmental intervention in the individual's choices among goods and services. Whatever conclusion you come to on this proposition, you should not fool yourself that economics and politics live on separate islands.

Those who would substitute the judgment of the bureaucrat for the judgment of the consumer inevitably forget that the free market for goods and the free market for ideas stem from the same root—freedom. They are inseparable. It was no accident that intellectual freedom disappeared under the Nazis and did not reappear until the free market system was reestablished in West Germany after the war. Russia and other Communist countries that control their economies also control their press and their professors. The road to serfdom is paved with the demands for governments to take over more and more economic activity.

Why the attitude is so persistent that business should not share freedom is somewhat of a mystery. The late Chet Huntley, a respected newscaster, wrote after his retirement:

> One general characteristic of the American press, which seems inexplicable, is the basic antipathy toward business and industry, which I believe exists in our journalism.

Huntley suggested that a possible reason for this perceived antipathy is the assumption by the press that business is more concerned with making money than providing the people with what they want. They forget that without money people cannot buy, and if people do not buy, there is no business or products or jobs or tax revenues. The tendency to deplore profits stems from the medieval idea that one person's profit is another person's loss. There is no question that there are shoddy practices in every profession and that our economy produces goods that are often vulgar or poorly made. The beauty of the system is that if the consumer doesn't want to buy certain goods, the businesses that produce them will either shift to new products or they will fail.

The critics of business labor under the illusion that they can draft a law to protect every right, defend every privilege, and anticipate every threat. When regulation fails, as it inevitably does, they do not repeal the laws but amend them into infinite complexity until the purpose of the original law is lost. The use of the regulatory reflex merely feeds an insatiable appetite for power on the part of an expanding government bureaucracy. We have now reached the point where one-sixth of the American labor force works for the government, and government expenditures are beyond 40 percent of the gross national product. Even some of the regulators are denouncing other regulators as barriers to better productivity.

The hand of government touches every aspect of human productivity. It is not only wasteful, but serves to destroy incentive and to discourage ingenuity. It is ironic that a society which looks to industry for the solution of many of its most pressing problems inhibits the ability of industry to respond. While present technology does not permit us to have surgically clean air and plentiful electricity at less cost at the same time, there is no reason to believe that future technology will not provide those benefits. The essential ingredient is freedom to act and an understanding that individual liberty is not only precious but efficient.

The time has come for businessmen to do two things—restudy the philosophy of free enterprise and recognize that they have the same rights under the First Amendment as any other group in our society.

The businessman, like the professor and the commentator, has the right under the First Amendment to express his views to the public and to his elected representatives. He is not a second-class citizen. Running a successful business enterprise calls for ethical men with the wisdom and patience to make prudent and responsible decisions in a highly competitive and fast-changing market.

There are overwhelming reasons for kinship, instead of hostility, between the free market for intellectual life and the free market for economic life. There is a similarity of interests: Both call for voluntary effort. Neither fraud nor coercion is within the ethics of the market system, since the competition of rivals provides alternatives to buyer and seller. So, too, free thought in our society is preserved by open competition among scholars. Just as thought control is the great enemy of freedom of inquiry in both the press and academia, economic controls are the great enemy of the entrepreneurial spirit.

Rediscovering the indivisibility of political and economic freedom will take time in a society that has become so accustomed to overreliance on government. The intellectual bias against the market is strongly entrenched, and there are some who always find a platform to continue to feed this bias out of hostility or a complete misunderstanding of the market function.

One of our least admired Presidents—Martin Van Buren —was characterized as one who approached power with muffled oars. Those who depend for existence on the First Amendment should sensitize their ears to pick up the sound of muffled oars seeking to approach power though a planned economy. That suggestion is in accordance with the sound liberal doctrine expressed by Woodrow Wilson: "The history of liberty is a history of limitations of governmental power, not the increase of it."

We should never forget that American life is a unique amalgam of political, religious, and economic pragmatism. Each sector contributes to, and indeed forms, part of the other sectors. An attack on one sector undermines the others. The lesson of history is that everything is connected to everything else.

The American press would not tolerate for one moment an attempt by the government to suppress news of riots or political demonstrations on the grounds that it wants to "ensure domestic tranquillity." The press knows a threat to the First Amendment when it sees one. However, when the government assumed the power to order what could be paid for our labor and what could be charged for products, on the grounds of "insuring price stability," the only question asked by most of the press was "Will it work?" That was the wrong question. The right question was "How did it affect individual liberty?" Is not one of the most basic human rights the right of a person to sell his or her labor at what the market will bring?

What really bothers me about price and wage controls is not only that they do not work, but the fact that 230 million fellow Americans have a tradition of inventing everything from the long rifle to the computer chip. They can figure out eighty ways around anything. It's destructive to our society for the executive branch to promulgate a law without benefit of legislative process, and then to say if you do not obey my law, I will penalize you by sending in the IRS, blocking government contracts, or whatever. If a definition of an imperial President is wanted, I can't think of anything more imperial. Once this process starts, disrespect for the law is built in over time.

Whatever the government—any government—decides to call its economic control methods does not really matter. Whether it's jawboning, incomes policy, voluntary guidelines, mandatory ceilings, or an economic police state, it means that the government threatens to hit you harder later on if you do not behave after it hits you the first time. History demonstrates that once a government picks up that club, it is very hard to put that club down again.

There are ten amendments in the Bill of Rights, although sometimes it seems that the press is so busy defending the first one that it is hard to get equal time for the other nine.

Let me recall one of them—the Ninth Amendment—which few people ever read anymore, let alone defend. It says:

> The enumeration in the Constitution, of certain rights, shall not be construed to deny or disparage others retained by the people.

For Americans, price controls and censorship of the press came into the world together. Both were expedients justified at the outset of World War II only by the overriding need for national survival. But those were simpler times. We began to experience events like Korea and Vietnam, which may have felt like war to soldiers but were officially labeled something else. And so the justification for expanding government controls became not just war, but "war or national emergency," and sometimes merely "national security."

The press has been vigilant in rebuffing the government's

efforts to impose the equivalent of wartime censorship under the flag of anything short of war. It stands up for the First Amendment, but it often remains silent about, or sometimes even greets with approval, the steady infringement of virtually every right that does not involve free speech. Justice Arthur Goldberg, in his opinion in *Griswold* v. *Connecticut* in 1965, put it this way:

> The Ninth Amendment to the Constitution may be regarded by some as a recent discovery and may be forgotten by others, but since 1791 it has been a basic part of the Constitution which we are sworn to uphold.

One of the great unreported stories of the past thirty years, in my view, is the steady erosion of individual rights that is turning us into a different kind of country. If you put a floor under wages and a ceiling over prices, a free man cannot long stand erect.

In talking about what "the government" is doing, it would be more accurate to speak of what we are doing to ourselves. The government adopts monetary policies and fiscal policies which produce inflation in response to popular demand. Since there is no "Truth in Politics" law, we must rely on the vigilance of the press to reveal the true costs of these policies. When we come to understand what is happening, I do not believe Americans are ready to sell their birthright of individual freedom. But someone has to make it clear that the collision course between government economic controls and personal liberty is inevitable because, in the end, government allocation of economic resources required force. Someone has to point out—and keep pointing out—that every time the tide recedes a little after one of those floods of "emergency" regulations, there is a little less sand left on the beach for free people to stand on.

If it finally gets down to a single grain, even though that grain is labeled "free speech and the First Amendment," you'll find that it isn't worth much.

The Law May Be Hazardous to Society's Health

■ ■ ■

All free societies that endure are based upon the rule of law; indeed, the dictum that we are "a government of laws and not of men" is embedded in the American consciousness. Democracy can be based on no other presumption. We are the masters, not the servants, of the state. The Declaration of Independence made this point with great clarity: Governments derive "their just powers from the consent of the governed," and further, "it is the right of the people to alter or to abolish" unsatisfactory procedures. Our first government failed, and in 1789 it was replaced by one based on the Constitution. Its first words state the thesis with maximum economy —We the people.

Unlike some revolutions, ours articulated a rationale that has stood the test of time and forms the basis for a free society. The assertion by the Declaration of Independence that the power of government derives from the consent of the governed depends upon a citizen being able to find out what his government is doing. Otherwise, consent is clearly impossible. Today, a good case can be made that no one knows, or can know, what our government is doing. Thus the legitimacy of its acts can no longer be supported by the consent of the governed. The same kind of proliferation of laws and regulations we are experiencing today was one of the complaints against George III enumerated in the Declaration of Independence. It specified that he "erected a multitude of new offices, and sent hither swarms of officers to harass our people, and eat out their substance." Our language today may not be as eloquent as Jefferson's but the thought is the same.

It has been said that if history never repeats itself, it at least offers parallels. From a part-time, one-man shop when first established in 1789, the Attorney General's office has grown into a vast nationwide bureaucracy with more than 56,000 employees and a three-billion-dollar annual budget.

Looking at our present legal and regulatory situation, one is reminded that ancient Rome started with laws consisting of Twelve Tables, which were committed to memory by school-children, but which ultimately grew to some three thousand brass plates deposited in the capitol and read by nobody. It cannot be said that this process caused the decline and fall of the Roman Empire, but it certainly did nothing to prevent it. Between the end and the beginning, Roman society evolved into one where, in Edward Gibbon's words:

> The civil jurisprudence . . . was . . . a mysterious science and a profitable trade, and the innate perplexity of the study was involved in tenfold darkness by the private industry of the practitioners. The expense of the pursuit sometimes exceeded the value of the prize.

It seems fair to say that what it took the Romans thirteen centuries to do, we have accomplished in only two. In fact, most of this has been achieved—if that's the right word—within the past eighty years. One of the reasons usually advanced for the legal avalanche is that life has become more complicated. We cannot expect to live in the 1980s according to rules that worked in the 1880s. No doubt the Romans were told something very similar. It was no more true then than it is now.

Anyone who thinks that the growth of government produced our social progress and vast improvements in the quality of life has lapsed into a logic fallacy known to Latin scholars as *post hoc, ergo propter hoc.* Freely translated, that means: "If one thing follows the other, it must have been caused by the other." If that were so, then the crowing of the rooster forces the sun to rise.

Social progress and the improvement of life are often the declared intentions of a government bureaucracy, but they certainly are not the results. To the contrary, most major advances proceed from areas of private initiative that government has not got around to stifling as yet.

Life's most important quality, health, has improved dramatically in the past four decades. Commonplace killers and cripplers like polio, smallpox, and tuberculosis are becoming dim memories as new medical resources and knowledge make ours the healthiest and longest-lived population ever. Government did not lead Jonas Salk to produce his vaccine, however. It merely stepped in and managed it after the fact.

Another key to the quality of life is what people do to earn a living. Millions who forty years ago would have strained their backs now exercise their brains and operate ingenious new machines, thanks to rapid advances in technology. But government did not invent these labor-saving devices and new technologies. It simply regulates some of them, and in so doing, retards their productivity.

In social progress, blacks, the elderly, women, and minorities now assume rights and opportunities barely dreamed of forty years ago. Government did not initiate this broadening of civil rights, however. Only when private individuals and groups demanded those rights—long and vigorously—did government yield and legislate them.

The heavy hand of bureaucracy rarely aids the advances made by individuals. More often it slows down that progress, or stops it altogether.

However the Romans accounted for their predicament, they presumably did not blame the invention of automobiles, airplanes, telephones, or intercontinental ballistic missiles. Nor is it likely that they attributed the need for regulation to the operations of J. Pierpont Morgan, Cornelius Vanderbilt, or John D. Rockefeller. Perhaps in Rome the emperor had a sinners' list of his own. If so, I'm sure it served the same useful purpose that such a list would have today—that is, invoking the evils of the past, real or imaginary, to gain acceptance for new laws and expanding authority for the lawmaker.

The old Romans were jealous of their freedom. But they failed to anticipate—and we have no excuse for not now anticipating—that when the laws became so numerous that even the lawyers could not keep up with them, their government could become as arbitrary as it liked, simply by deciding which laws to enforce and which to ignore. This process continued until, according to Gibbon, their government finally "united the evils of liberty and servitude, and the Romans were oppressed at the same time by the multiplicity of their laws and the arbitrary will of their masters."

In short, government authority no longer rested on the consent of the governed.

That we are perilously close to that point in late-twentieth-century America seems almost self-evident. While new technology is not responsible for this, it provides some new refinements. There are now, for instance, some four billion records on individuals stored in the data systems of some ninety-seven federal agencies. A push of the button can produce a complete picture of the financial, medical, political, and personal life of almost any one of us. Since it is impossible to process simultaneously the records of 230 million Americans, who gets singled out for special attention comes to depend more and more on the whim of the button pusher. That is not government by law; it is government by men, and what is true for individuals is also true for corporations, universities, associations, or any other organization.

Citicorp spends sixteen million dollars a year in legal fees, and it is a possibility that we might be in conformity with every law or regulation affecting the banking business—but only a possibility. Every now and then the bank is accused of an obscure offense that it did not even realize existed, despite floors of lawyers working full time to try to ensure our conformity. Still, the bank can slip up on something as commonplace as the film in a surveillance camera running out, which is a violation, because the branch manager was too busy taking care of his customers to check on it.

Since the web of laws is now so pervasive, it puts the power of selective enforcement in the hands of the bureaucrat, a politician running for office, or an investigative reporter looking for a story. Billy Carter, brother of the former President, found out that not having his fire extinguisher charged was a violation of the law, but millions remain in ignorance of that important fact because the ordinary worker has no news value. A dim bulb in the taillight of your car can fail to pass the legal screen. Farmers have been made to carry their federal marketing cards, aliens their visas, workers their social security cards, travelers their passports, and poultry handlers, architects, tattoo artists, photographers, miners, and social workers their licenses. A government permit has become necessary for everything from getting married to hiking in the wilderness.

The list could run on forever. It is so long that no index can be made just listing the subjects covered, let alone what the law says.

It would be tragic if what began as the rule of law was in the end brought down through the sheer confusion that the mass of law now creates. As more and more laws and regulations are put on the books each day, more and more people have to ignore them. We are training an entire generation that, with some justification, can have little respect for the law. We are suffocating voluntarism under a blanket of laws, rules, and regulations. Our free society, which is rooted in voluntary compliance, stands in danger of strangulation.

We are a nation of immigrants who voted with their feet that America was their voluntary choice. Voluntarism thus became the rock on which we all stand. Immigration is only one evidence of voluntarism, but a powerful one. In no other country in the world do men and women move so freely from place to place and from one occupation to another. We are the most mobile society in all history, and no other nation can match the American people in the multiplicity of voluntary societies for every form of social welfare. Those voluntary associations do society's work through the unpaid work of free citizens. It is a system that has worked for America. The great judge Learned Hand put it succinctly:

> Our democracy rests upon the assumption that set free, the common man can manage his own fate; that errors will cancel each other by open discussion; that the interest of each, even when unguided from above, will not diverge too radically from the interests of all.

The implementation of that philosophy has produced the most productive society the world has ever known, evidenced not only by our national outpouring of goods and services but also by the large measure of individual freedom we all enjoy. The framework that supports our unique society is that, until fairly recently, most of us voluntarily conformed to the law. Unfortunately for all, such voluntary conformity is becoming literally impossible for the majority of the American people.

Surely, a precondition for voluntary conformity is knowledge of at least the broad outlines of the law, but in America today, only the very rich or the very poor have any possibility whatsoever of learning what the law is. There are so many laws, and regulations with the force of law, that it is a fair bet everyone reading this book is in violation of some statute, myself included. We just do not know which one. Nor can most individuals afford to find out. The poor man learns about the law with a nightstick across his head. The rich are able to hire enough lawyers to advise them on at least some of the laws and regulations that pour out of government at all levels. The big corporation learns about it from a headline in the papers: "X Corporation Violates Y Law."

For all their insight, the framers of our Constitution could not foresee a day when 535 legislators would employ a staff of 25,000 aides to assist them in their legislative tasks. One of the horde of Senate aides, Michael Scully, wrote in *The Public Interest:*

> The real question is not who runs the Senate but rather which group—the elected or the unelected—dominates the operations: Senators, by being elected, or staff, by being numerous.

His question is sharpened when we read in the *Congressional Record* that a number of senators often request permission for unelected staff members to attend the business of the greatest deliberative body in the world on their behalf.

Our Founding Fathers could have told their successors that such a horde would propose far too much legislation. There are, in fact, about twenty thousand bills introduced in Congress annually—almost one for each staff member, by an odd coincidence. On a single day not long ago, no fewer than 272 committees and subcommittees of the Congress were in session, and at the end of that day, the President of the United States signed 843 laws.

On a typical day, the *Federal Register* prints 300,000 words, each one of which is amending or putting out a new regulation. Who can read 300,000 words a day? I don't know how long *Gone With the Wind* is, but it can't be much more than that. I, for one, could not read that in a single day, though it is surely far better reading than the *Federal Register.*

In one year there appeared in the *Federal Register* 175 new rules and 2,865 proposed amendments to existing rules. By that year's end, 309 final rules and 7,305 rule amendments were promulgated. There was a synergism there rarely equaled in other fields, if ever.

All this hyperactivity at the federal level must then be multiplied by fifty to get the true impact of our penchant for legislative overkill. In just one year more than 45,000 bills were introduced in the fifty state legislatures. In my own state alone, New York, 20,000 of them were introduced and the New York Legislature passed 2,000. The governor mitigated the effect somewhat—he signed only 1,800.

In New York City, suffering from urban decay and desperately needing new housing, the building code consists of 843 pages, and it requires that every builder obtain anywhere from 40 to 130 different building permits and licenses.

So it is very simple to say that someone broke the law! But I will hazard a guess that there is no one yet who has read those 1,800 laws, including the members of the New York Legislature who passed them, or read the New York City Building Code, much less anyone who makes the *Federal Register* daily reading.

Obviously, we have ignored the warning uttered long ago by Spinoza: "He who tries to fix and determine everything by law will inflame rather than correct the vices of the world."

Exhibit A is the Truth-in-Lending Act, a great title that implies that prior to its passage in 1968 the truth was hard to find. By 1977, the fifty-three sections of that law had been interpreted forty-three times by the Board of Governors of the Federal Reserve, no doubt practicing law without a license. Their pronouncements have been revised in the light of some twelve hundred staff letters of further interpretation. The result is six thousand pages of regulations. In addition, there are parallel state laws: no fewer than seven in the State of New York governing your MasterCard bill. One delineates the size of the type in the text of the bill. Another specifies the length of the text and states that if the type is smaller than a certain size the contract is not enforceable in court. Still another delineates what must go on the front of the bill and what must go on the back. I commend Spinoza's advice to the well-meaning but misguided authors of all these laws and regulations, and I would point out that 90 percent of the banks in the United States have fewer than two hundred employees. There is no way the small banks can read those six thousand pages of Federal Reserve regulations, much less all the applicable state statutes. Consequently, at one point there were ten thousand lawsuits in courts throughout the United States based on Truth-in-Lending laws. You don't have ten thousand lawsuits if everyone agrees on what the law is.

Overregulation is partly our own fault. We let something run wide open until the law of compensating forces operates. Businessmen sometimes fail to anticipate or even respond to the demands of the consumer. If that continues too long, the public becomes angry. Typically, then, the industry or the labor union that is perceived to be out of control forms a "self-regulating" group to set standards and police its own activity. Those self-regulatory groups usually fail to respond quickly and strongly enough, so that pressure continues to mount and the government steps in. Lawyers who let some of their brethren disrupt the decorum of the courtroom without effective censure are moving into that zone of trouble. So, too, are those bar associations that see nothing wrong with publicly recommending people as judges before whom the members themselves will soon practice. Failure to reform themselves, or to perceive how rapidly our value systems change, will create volumes of regulations that we will all live to regret.

The legal precedent upon which much of our regulation is still based was established in 1670, when Lord Chief Justice Matthew Hale declared that "property does become clothed with a public interest, when used in a manner to make it of public consequence, and affect the community at large." Defining the public interest in precise terms has occupied the time and attention of generations of judges and lawyers, economists and accountants, businessmen, labor leaders, and politicians, at a cost of billions of dollars to government and industry. With the passage of time, the doctrine of public interest has become buried beneath an avalanche of charges and briefs, statistics and analyses.

The regulator is always adjured to serve the public interest. Sooner or later, the regulatory body makes rules with the force of law, and an administrative judge, who is often an officer of the regulatory body, then becomes prosecutor, judge, and jury all at the same time. The regulatory body substitutes its opinion for the judgment of the free market. As time goes on, the bureaucracy changes the active verb "to compete" into the passive "to be regulated." This process tends to create a rigid, backward-looking system which is neither business-oriented nor consumer-oriented. Instead it is bureaucracy-oriented.

Time and again when there is opportunity to introduce a new technology, or a new service to meet public need, the regulator's first question is not whether the consumer or the public will be better served, but whether what is new fits into the regulatory pattern. Can it be regulated? Will it require a new statute? Does it call for a shift in policy? The result has often been that what the regulator cannot regulate he will not approve.

Many industries continue to be regulated as though they were monopolies, when in fact new competitors have long since taken away a good share of their business. Free competition, which grows up outside the reach of the regulator, creates a whole new situation, with the odds heavily stacked against the regulated. Instead of welcoming the competitive challenge posed by new industries or applauding the new benefits to the public, the regulatory reflex is to reach out and regulate the new lot too, permitting no industry to either win or lose on its merits, but causing the public to pay the check for poorer service and higher costs.

Creativity, particularly the invention and application of new technology, requires brains, capital, and hard work. Reward runs with risk, but the regulatory system is not receptive to change. Talented people, therefore, move on to areas where talent is rewarded. With some notable exceptions, the history of railroad regulation is a classic example of this. It also demonstrates opposition to change through improved technology.

Before the Interstate Commerce Commission clapped the railroads into a regulatory straitjacket, railroads were pioneers in technology, creating the standard track gauge, new freight cars, and safety devices. One of the first acts of the ICC was to tell the railroads that rails should be made of domestic iron and not imported steel, which at the time was far more durable. Time after time, the efforts of the railroads to improve efficiency through the introduction of new and applied technology were hampered by infuriating and costly delays in regulatory decisions. The regulators expended their efforts in setting tariffs that distinguished between horses for slaughter and horses for draft, between rates for sand used for cement and sand used in glassmaking. This bureaucratic concern with trivial instead of key issues at a time of trouble can only be compared to the steward's obsession with rearranging the deck chairs while the *Titanic* was sinking. Predictably, many railroads chugged slowly down the road to ruin.

By what route have we arrived at this danger point for human freedom? If we look closely at where we are now in our national journey, I think it can be argued that, almost without being aware of it, we have ignored the basic intention of the Founding Fathers to achieve a fair and equitable government through the checks and balances prescribed in the Constitution. The constitutions of some of the original states, notably those of Virginia, Maryland, and Massachusetts, provided specifically for the separation of powers between the executive, legislative, and judicial branches.

The separation-of-powers concept was nailed to the mast by John Adams in the Massachusetts Constitution of 1780:

> In the government of this commonwealth, the legislative department shall never exercise the executive and judicial powers, or either of them; the executive shall never exercise the legislative and judicial powers, or either of them; the judicial shall never exercise the legislative and executive powers, or either of them; to the end that it may be a government of laws and not of men.

That may sound tedious, but its clarity is classic. The framers of the U.S. Constitution incorporated that basic doctrine, though not in so doctrinaire a form. In the *Federalist Papers,* James Madison said with emphasis that the separation, though not absolute, must be observed.

Current practice violates not only the letter but the spirit of the principle. We have ignored John Locke's dictum that "the legislative cannot transfer the power of making laws to any other hands, for it being but a delegated power from the people, they who have it cannot pass it over to others."

Between 1970 and 1975, seven major federal regulatory agencies were created by Congress, further eroding the doctrine of the separation of powers. Over the same period, thirty major laws were enacted making substantive changes in the regulatory framework. The executive, in the form of regulatory agencies, now fills the *Federal Register* day after day with explicit evidence that the separation of powers has eroded to such an extent as to constitute a clear and present danger.

We are moving toward the kind of society described by de Tocqueville as one advancing toward despotism. That is one, he said, which "covers the surface of society with a network of small, complicated rules, minute and uniform, through which the most original minds and the most energetic characters cannot penetrate. . . . The will of men is not shattered but softened, bent and guided." The lines between the three divisions of function in government have become so blurred that one is tempted to long for the overexplicitness of John Adams.

Our Constitution says clearly that all bills for raising revenue shall originate in the House of Representatives. It is no secret that since the Budget Act of 1921, the reality is that such bills originate with the executive. A delegate to the Constitutional Convention, who through some miracle might return to earth two centuries later, would be appalled to learn that a federal judge appointed and controlled the principal and teachers of South Boston High School, to say nothing of laboring over maps to lay out bus routes. No matter what the perceived social justification for such actions, they transgress the doctrine of the separation of powers and confuse the legislative, judicial, and executive functions.

We have so fouled our nest that federal agencies of the executive branch issue subpoenas of more than one thousand pages calling for data that must be measured in miles of computer tape.

Complex interpretations of law, bizarre as they are, are not the fault of the regulatory agencies. The fault is the direct result of Congress delegating the legislative functions to the executive. The bureaucracy has become so proliferous, its discretion so broad, its rules so unstable, that there is a strong tendency to make this a government of men, not of laws.

The area of ignorance, or noncompliance, or both, is not limited to the private sector. Indeed, it flourishes in the public sector. Not only does the public sector have all the problems of trying to find out what the law is, but more confusion arises when one regulatory body attempts to enforce its rules on another. Public bodies often have goals set for them by legislation that is in conflict with the goals of other public bodies set by the same legislature. Everyone in the private sector has to pay attention to even the lowest-ranking member of the bureaucracy lest he have a contract canceled, be subjected to a well-publicized legal threat, or suffer an unfair press leak. Win, lose, or draw, the bureaucracy will remain forever, but the private company may be driven out of business.

Federal agencies are not subject to those modern forms of imperial intimidation and tend to ignore other regulators. Why the law is difficult, if not impossible, to enforce in the public sector was spelled out by James Q. Wilson and Patricia Rachal. "Inside government," they wrote, "there is very little sovereignty, only rivals and allies." The private sector cannot deny the authority of the state, but a government agency can and does deny the authority of another agency.

Ernesto Angelo, when he was the mayor of Midland, Texas, understood that better than most. When the federal Department of Housing and Urban Development applied for a parking space at the municipal airport, Mayor Angelo returned the application with a request for more information. The first requirement, Mr. Angelo told the Feds, was to obtain from the U.S. Government Printing Office, the National Archives, the Library of Congress, or someplace, a supply of application forms COM 1975. Then they were to print three executed copies and fourteen confirmed copies. Next they were asked to submit the make and model of the proposed vehicle, along with certified assurance that everyone connected with the manufacture and service of said vehicle had been paid according to a wage scale that complies with the Davis-Bacon Act. The next requirement was a genealogical table for everyone who would operate the vehicle, so Midland could ascertain that there would be a precisely equal percentage of whites, blacks, and other minorities, as well as women and the elderly, driving the vehicle. HUD may still be filling out the forms.

The chances of this state of disorder changing is remote, but the reality of the public sector growing is certain. That being so, more and more citizens, even those on the public payroll, will fail to obey the law. When government itself is contemptuous of law, no citizen is likely to respect its authority.

James Madison accurately foretold this moment in history when he wrote in the *Federalist Papers:*

> It will be of little avail to the people that laws are made by men of their choice, if the laws be so voluminous that they cannot be read, or so incoherent that they cannot be understood . . . or undergo such incessant change that no man who knows what the law is today can guess what it will be tomorrow.

Few would dispute that we have now arrived at the point in our national journey that Madison warned us against. It would be a supreme irony if Congress, which talks so much about the citizen's right to know, makes effective knowledge absolutely impossible by passing so many prolix laws.

The weight of the vast bureaucracy, created by law and, in turn, creating new laws, is now so oppressively heavy it cannot be ignored.

In a voluntary society, reform must start at the local level. Each of us must use our influence and persuasive powers to save our free society. Take a leaf from the book of our forefathers and stand up and be counted. They pledged their lives, their fortunes, and their sacred honor—in short, everything they had—to found this country. Our society is now infinitely more complex, infinitely more dangerous, and inextricably bound up with the rest of the world. Nevertheless, with the bureaucratic balance moving against us, with a rapidly aging industrial plant, with the heavy hand of regulation effectively closing every avenue to free American innovation, capital formation, energy, and skills, the time is growing late.

Yet the pendulum does swing, and there is always something each of us can do to help the process. In London, Big Ben once had a tray on its pendulum where stacks of old English pennies were placed to regulate the clock. If there is anyone who thinks he or she may have a few cents to add, I can only suggest that now is a very good time to do it.

My own two cents worth is to call for the majority of laws to expire by their own terms, or to make zero-based laws, open at any moment to the query: Why did we need it in the first place? If it was useful then, is it still an imperative necessity?

If that movement gathered momentum, it would help, but we need something more. The one law not subject to interpretation or mutation, even by the Supreme Court, is Parkinson's Second Law: Work expands to fill the time available. It used to be that the Congress was in session about three months each year. The rest of the time members were home listening to the people who elected them. Today, Congress meets almost twelve months of the year, with a few recesses, leaving a staff of twenty-five thousand to dream up new laws to bring voluntary compliance to the breaking point. Senator Howard Baker recalls that when his father was elected to Congress in 1950, Congress was in session an average of one hundred and three days. The senator does not accept the argument that present problems are so radically different as to require the abandonment of our American tradition of citizen legislators in favor of the elected bureaucracy Congress has now become.

It seems to me it is time for a more drastic proposal. Let us have a constitutional amendment that would limit the congressional session to six or seven months. Parkinson's law would still work, but with a little luck, we can cut down the number of new laws. Even a slowdown in the rate of increase might buy some time for our voluntary democracy. A shorter session and more contact with the electorate—and less with the staff and the Washington press corps—might restore some sense of perspective to our legislative process. The same result could be achieved by a simple majority vote at the beginning of each new Congress, but that would require a fresh vote each session.

That modern Delphic oracle, the public opinion poll, which legislators now rely on instead of actually talking to real live constituents, has diagnosed the syndrome. Over the last decade the polls have indicated that more and more people believe that the part of their personal lives over which they are permitted to exercise some control is rapidly diminishing. We have all become suspicious of authority, at every level. A majority of us must now ignore the law because there is no other viable alternative. Surely this condition is a warning signal for society.

It is time to act. It is time to curb the proliferation of laws lest they smother our legal system. To those who say this is too large a task, I would quote Justice Brandeis, who summarized the issue in three sentences: "Those who won our independence were not cowards. They did not fear political change. They did not exalt order at the cost of liberty."

If we continue to force an increasing majority of our population to ignore the law, we shall have neither order nor liberty, and we will run the risk that an authoritarian government will fill the void.

Going to Hell on
a Best-Fit Curve

· ■ ·

O ne of the more difficult mental feats to which we can
subject ourselves is trying to recall what we were thinking about a year ago, five years ago, and ten years ago. What
were the great events, the human triumphs, the impending
disasters of these points in time? The velocity of events is so
enormous, and the rate of change in the world so great, that
it is hard to recall, out of the endless stream of data, what we
were all concentrating on only yesterday. Add to this the fact
that most of the great achievements of mankind are won
slowly and are not the stuff of headlines, while the crises—by
definition—come upon us suddenly. It then becomes clear
why we find it hard to maintain the perspective necessary for
a balanced view of what is happening in the world around us
at any given moment.

Each of us is the product of unique personal experience
that remains very limited even when supplemented by study
of past events as described by others. From the perspective of
a person situated by fate in the midst of a multinational corporation, I have watched or been involved, at least on the margin, in many situations that were touted at the time as
harbingers of disaster. These events have ranged from the rise

of the popular front in France after World War II, which was greeted by many pundits of that day as the inevitable forerunner of an all-Communist Europe, to recurring press reports now that all less developed countries are about to go bankrupt and bring the world's financial system down with them.

Anyone who has been involved in some collective decision, great or small, knows that the outcome is usually determined by a narrow margin and at least a measure of good luck. But since history is rarely written about what does not happen, most of the literature leaves the reader with a sense that the outcome was inevitable. As George Gilder has put it:

> To many people the past seems inevitable and the future impossible. History is seen to have arisen not from unpredictable flows of genius and heroism, but more or less inevitably, from preordained patterns of natural resources and population.

Contemporary newscasters select a few events from among the millions occurring on our globe and present them in twenty-two minutes on the seven o'clock news. This compression of events is not as distorted as some narrative works that cover the history of a century in two sentences. But it illustrates why it is so hard to learn from history. Regression analyses of historical data rarely validate extrapolation because most history is never written down. It is literally impossible to obtain enough data, not only on events but on man's motives, to make an extrapolation valid. The best-fit curve, so useful in engineering, cannot be laid out in human affairs because we simply do not have enough data points. William Irwin Thompson put it this way:

> One can say almost anything about human culture now and it will be true, for everything is going on at once . . . from the disappearance of the nation-state to the explosion of nationalism in Quebec, Wales, Scotland, and the land of the Basques; from the appearance of a

new radicalism to the resurgence of a new conservatism; from a planetary miscegenation to a new tribal racism.

When one reflects on this summary, which is by no means complete, we see that any account, any number of data points, is an oversimplification. This can be illustrated by a recent personal experience—either yours or mine. Each of us who voted in a presidential election recently may have had slightly different reasons to pull the lever we did. Despite this, some columnists now tell the world we voted for new leaders with a new agenda, while others, using the same data, assure us that all we did was vote against the incumbent. Before the widespread use of movable type and the printing press, even less data were captured, but the results of extrapolation were about the same. People simply rushed to unwarranted conclusions using less scientific methods.

Our inability to predict what will happen tomorrow with any accuracy is fortunately offset by man's ability to cope with the unpredictable. This is a recurring theme in the long history of mankind, and the major reason we have survived. Since we are the prisoners of what we know, often we are unable even to imagine what we don't know. The most qualified *expert* is, in fact, likely to be the most hidebound, and even the free-wheeling science fiction writer often falls short.

The cartoons of Buck Rogers appearing in the newspapers in the 1930s turned out to be remarkably similar to what American astronauts wore when they actually landed on the moon. No one was greatly surprised by the success of the moon shot. The dream of a moon voyage runs back through history. Indeed, the event itself was widely anticipated. But the dean of science fiction writers, Isaac Asimov, reminds us that not one of the writers had predicted the most remarkable thing about the event—that when it happened the whole world would be watching on television.

The use of a group of experts to study and predict has a long tradition in man's history. Such commissions often have an enviable record of telling us what happened, and why, but a lamentable score when they proceed from there to telling us what will happen next.

In 1486, King Ferdinand and Queen Isabella set up a committee, headed by Fray Hernanco de Talavera, to study Columbus's plan for reaching the Indies by sailing west. After four years' work the committee reported that such a voyage was impossible because: one, the western ocean is infinite and unnavigable; two, if Columbus reached the Antipodes he could not get back; and three, there are no Antipodes because the greater part of the globe is covered with water, as St. Augustine said much earlier.

Not long ago, the doom and gloom Club of Rome sold a lot of newspapers, and the book *Small Is Beautiful* flirted with the best-seller list. Both were repackaging for our century of Thomas Malthus's view of the eighteenth. Malthus had no computer, but he managed to extrapolate the future solely from current data. Noting that population increased geometrically, while food supply appeared to increase in arithmetic progression, Malthus hurled some nightmarish statistics at society. In 1798, he gave the world twenty-five years before it would engage in a grim struggle for survival.

Even as he wrote, what historians would later call the Industrial Revolution was gathering force, and with it a new era of mechanized agriculture, chemical fertilizers, and plant genetics which would make scientific farming one of the most productive occupations of our time.

About the only thing that can be stated with any degree of confidence about human events is that whatever we are most concerned about today is a poor guide to tomorrow's problems, except perhaps in an inverse ratio.

Pessimism, of course, did not die out with the advance of science and industry. Mankind's great leaps forward carried the doomsayers along with the optimists. Myopia is just as common in the twentieth century as it was in past eras.

Just before Pearl Harbor, learned men drew attention to the fact that Japan depended on the United States for 80 percent of its gasoline, so war was not only unlikely but impossible. On the other side of the world, an ambassador was reported in *Time* magazine as saying: Hitler told me that conquest of the western hemisphere by German armies was as fantastic as an invasion of the moon. Charles A. Lindbergh, after inspecting the German air force, was convinced no country could withstand Göring's air superiority, and used the radio to urge American isolationism. All of them made the same basic mistake as the doomsayers, even if some of them came out on the optimistic side.

The shock of the Japanese attack, when it came, was great. It took three years for the tide of that war to turn, and when it did, Allied air power and rapid innovation were the decisive factors. The technical ingenuity that created synthetic rubber and radar during the war played a more important part in its outcome than the development of the atomic bomb.

When at last the war was over, many experts predicted a great postwar depression. They were not mere theorists; they had witnessed the First World War and knew from experience what had to happen next. One major corporation, acting on that belief, did nothing but pile up cash against the inevitable crash that never came. Up to today, that company has not recovered its competitive position.

When the Marshall Plan was proposed in 1947, pessimists predicted it would never work. Politicians warned against pouring more U.S. tax dollars "down the European rat hole" and urged a return to isolationism. Decimated Europe, and some voices in high places in America, demanded punishment for Germany and Italy, rather than aid. Fortunately, the United States had learned something from the economic catastrophe that followed World War I. We underwrote the recovery of both our enemies and our allies, thus avoiding the burdensome structure of reparations and debt that had doomed economic prosperity after Versailles. The coping mechanism worked.

The Marshall Plan sent a flow of investment capital from America, where it had been created. Despite repeated forecasts that the "dollar gap" was structural and thus beyond the capacity of Europe to redress, a free and expansive system of interdependent markets got under way.

The dimensions of the recovery were astounding. In five years European industrial production rose 248 percent and the dollar gap narrowed by 80 percent.

In 1952, even the optimists failed to predict the economic miracles getting under way in Germany and Japan. To a great extent, Germany prospered by rejecting the advice of American experts, abolished controls and confiscatory taxation, and let individual initiative take over. As the global economy embarked upon a period of unprecedented expansion and prosperity, there were still doomsayers who anticipated economic collapse around every corner and perceived each problem as a full-blown crisis. Instant communications systems, which sped the world's growth, just as rapidly circulated rumors of its imminent demise.

In the midst of the economic miracle, a new cult of concern was led by an articulate Frenchman. "The American Challenge," of the 1960s, described by Jean-Jacques Servan-Schreiber as breaking down the "political framework" of Europe and plunging Europeans into "total despair," simply did not materialize. Multinational drive, if anything, reversed direction. American sovereignty in the 1980s is no more likely to be lost to foreign investment than was Europe's in the 1960s. But the world moves on to new concerns.

The neo-Malthusian "Limits to Growth" crisis that burst upon the '70s with such dismal force lost credibility as sensible people discovered that the Club of Rome's computer was not programmed to include real-world variables, such as human ingenuity. The club's follow-up reports, grudgingly admitting that some growth is both necessary and possible, were less publicized. The same was true of Malthus two centuries ago.

Few people know that Malthus revised his thesis in 1803 to allow that man could influence his own fate by, for instance, preventive checks on population growth. Despite his second thoughts, his original doomsday scenario became so embedded in nineteenth-century thought that for decades the misery of the poor was considered necessary and poverty deemed ineradicable. Malthus's projections were said to be partly responsible for William Pitt's withdrawing a proposed poor law that might have given the poverty-stricken an economic leg up. Instead, England instituted the harsh and punitive workhouse system, well known to readers of Charles Dickens.

It is a memorable illustration of how the power of an idea, even when wrong, can influence our action when endlessly reported.

A recent example is the OPEC price embargo. This event set off a round of price increases that quadrupled the cost of oil. No thoughtful person could fail to understand that there had occurred a fundamental change in the calculus of world economics. We were told to prepare for a global catastrophe, as oil-importing nations would surely fail to meet their increased debts. Armageddon was at hand for industrial civilization. That view was summed up by a panel of international experts in the quarterly *Foreign Affairs:*

> Whether this [will] result in currency devaluation, in default by banks and businesses . . . or in political revolution and debt repatriation, the entire structure of world payments, and of trade and financial relationships [will] certainly be fractured.

Nothing of the sort happened. Thanks to free-floating Eurodollars, global data nets, and thousands of participants pressing their own economic intents, the world had become one huge financial marketplace and the market was able to handle it. New OPEC surpluses were recycled through the Euromarket and lent to other countries, especially to less-developed countries in need of funds to meet increased oil bills. The enormous efficiency of the marketplace handled these transfers with very minor casualties. This gave individual countries the time to adjust their policies to take into account the new realities. Ten years later, current account deficits of the LDCs in real terms are about the same as they were before the embargo, and their international reserves have actually increased.

The real news today is that life is much better for the mass of the world's population than in any period in history. In some of the LDCs the standard of living has doubled in the last ten years. This is a feat that even the most dedicated optimist could not have predicted and the pessimists have still not recognized.

To observe that mankind has been able to build a continuously better life on this planet is not to say that the world is not complex and often dangerous. The doomsayers have always had their uses, since they trigger the coping mechanism that often prevents the events they forecast. Indeed, it was only when the Greeks made critics legitimate that old shibboleths fell and fresh ideas sparked new progress. A century ago, the world's scientific knowledge doubled about every fifty years; in 1960, it doubled every ten years; and it doubles now every five. While no one knows if this rate can continue, it is clearly increasing the quantity of unknown variables. It is the kind of thing that should give pause to the forecasters; should, but I doubt that it will even slow them down.

Of course, we have another option: we can reject the future altogether and cling to the past. We can emulate members of the Flat Earth Research Society, who have never quite given up hope. The society, founded in 1800, still claims nearly two thousand tenacious believers, who dismissed the moon shot as an "elaborate hoax."

All of this reinforces the conclusion of the great historian Carl Becker, who summed up a lifetime of scholarship with the observation: "In human affairs nothing is predetermined until after it has occurred." Mindful of his warning, I unhesitatingly tell you that the world is round and that it is much better off economically than many would have us think. Both the optimists and the doomsayers have a role to play, but the heavy lifting will be done by men and women who day in, day out work to advance the cause of mankind. They are the people who have always made the coping mechanism work and moved society forward. They can be relied upon to continue doing so in the future.

THE
BUSINESS/GOVERNMENT
CONNECTION

■ ■ ■

Banking in Wonderland

■

To understand what's going on in the banking business in the United States, which you should because it's your money, it is necessary to take a cue from a certain professor of mathematics at Oxford.

His name was Charles Lutwidge Dodgson and he was noted in academic circles of his time as the author of *Euclid and His Modern Rivals* as well as for other abstruse mathematical works. He is far more widely known by his nom de plume, Lewis Carroll, and over many years millions have delighted in his better-known work, *Alice in Wonderland.* Though he wrote *Alice* to amuse a six-year-old girl, I sometimes think Professor Dodgson was really prophesying the shape of the U.S. banking system, which defies comprehension in rational terms.

Imagine, then, as you read this, that a white rabbit with pink eyes appears, pulls a watch from his waistcoat, and leads us all through the looking glass into a wonderland called the American banking system.

In Wonderland, you will recall, logic never seems to work quite the same way as it does in, say, Wisconsin, and things are never quite what they seem. So it is also in banking and the financial services markets. For example, it is an article of faith that American banks do not compete across state lines; that certain kinds of banks do not compete with other kinds; that stockbrokers do not offer banking services; that insurance companies do not sell stocks; or that retailers and steelmakers do none of those things. In banking wonderland, everything is neatly compartmentalized in theory, but actuality is another matter entirely.

It's as if the March Hare, or is it the Mad Hatter, is running around shouting, "No room! No room!" at the tea party when in fact there is clearly room for everybody. But, like Alice, Americans have "got so much in the way of expecting nothing but out-of-the-way things to happen, that it [seems] quite dull . . . for life to go on in the common way."

So no one is astonished to open the newspaper and discover that the major New York commercial banks are in head-on competition with the First Nationwide Savings, a thrift institution with 140 offices coast to coast, which the courts and the regulators assure us does not compete with commercial banks, and certainly not across state lines, except that it does but apparently hasn't yet been enlightened to that fact. To compound your confusion, I might point out that the organization I headed before retirement, technically a New York–based one-bank holding company, now operates savings and loan organizations in Florida, Illinois, and California. These have been blessed by the courts and regulators and are perfectly legal—illogical, perhaps, but legal.

If you asked me to explain this, since I am not an Oxford mathematician I would have to say, as Alice did to the Caterpillar, "I'm afraid I can't put it more clearly, for I can't understand it myself to begin with."

It can be described, however, and the place to begin is at the beginning.

Our banking system is a part of our frontier heritage. Whenever the wagon trains stopped to water the horses, a couple of guys dropped out and opened a bank. That is why the United States today has more than 14,000 banks, 3,800 savings and loan associations, 430 mutual savings banks, and 21,000 credit unions. Unlike Canada, Great Britain, and most other nations, where fewer than a dozen large banks operate nationwide, we have a grand total of 41,591 depository institutions that will take your money for safekeeping, pay you a rent called interest for the use of your money, and then lend it to a third party—if possible, at a rate sufficiently higher than the rent to cover their costs of operation and, if managed properly, make a profit to finance their future growth.

Most of these depository institutions are small. Ninety-five percent of the more than fourteen thousand commercial banks in the United States have fewer than two hundred employees and assets of less than three million dollars, which is a small number in the banking business. Many still reflect a nineteenth-century image in their buildings and style of operations, as well as in their thinking. Outside they look like fortresses; inside they are public palaces. Lavish interiors give customers something to admire while waiting in endless lines as tellers cash checks, take deposits, and record all transactions by hand, despite the popularity of automated teller machines which give faster, more efficient service. Too many banks are still rooted in the nineteenth century, when bankers, who would not tolerate sloppy penmanship, proudly boasted that their account books were works of art and employees worked long hours and had to adhere to strict moral standards. The following set of rules, found in Citibank's archives, was typical of nineteenth-century banking:

> The office will open at 7 A.M. and close at 8 P.M. daily except on the Sabbath. Each employee is expected to spend the Sabbath attending church.

> Each clerk will bring in a bucket of water and a scuttle of coal for the day.

> Make your pens carefully. Whittle the nibs to suit your taste.

> Men employees will be given an evening off each week for courting purposes, or two evenings if they regularly go to church.

Any employee who smokes Spanish cigars, uses liquor in any form, gets shaved at a barber shop, or frequents pool or public halls, will give us good reason to suspect his worth, intentions, integrity and honesty.

The employee who has performed his labor faithfully and without fault for a period of five years in our service, and is looked upon by his fellow men as a law-abiding citizen, will be given an increase of ten cents per day in his pay.

The steady technological progress we have seen in this century seemed to have had little effect on many banks. Still relying on the old ways, these banks preferred to compete among themselves, and with other, nonfinancial institutions, by offering the customer a wide range of free services. In the 1920s, for instance, banks acted as railroad and theater ticket agents, made hotel reservations, maintained day nurseries for tired mothers, distributed seeds, and some even kept veterinarians on the payroll.

Things did not change much for a long time. Until quite recently, any time a bank wanted to run up its deposits, it offered toasters or blankets as premiums for opening a new account. A ten-dollar toaster hardly made up for the rip-off that was forced on consumers from 1965 to 1982; Regulation Q provided that the poor got 5.25 percent on their savings and the rich got 12 to 14 percent or more. The difference in dollars is not inconsiderable. In the first two years after Reg Q ended, banks paid an additional seventy billion dollars in interest on savings accounts at the new market rates. This consumer rip-off was just incredible and it went on for seventeen years, even though there are a lot more savers in this country than there are borrowers. Anyone with a sense of fair play would agree that the working-man should get the same market rate on his savings account that the rich man gets on his. But in cohoots with the government, the small banks and savings and loan institutions were happy to pay the lowest possible rate to savers. In turn, they lent money to local businesses, often at high rates that made competitive big-city banks green with envy. They bought government bonds with their surplus and they did very well indeed. They liked it that way and did not want things to change, and they succeeded at preserving the status quo long after the twin forces of inflation and technology reshaped the marketplace. Even now ignoring reality, banking continues to be hobbled in its ability to compete on equal terms with all comers as a result of rigid regulations, which suit the small banks and thrifts just fine.

The end result was predictable. Regulation Q, originally laid on at the behest of the savings and loan associations to give them an edge over banks, drove savings into market rate alternatives. Money market mutual funds grew to about four billion dollars in three years from the time the first one was founded, and then soared to over two hundred billion dollars in the next five years. To give you a time frame for that, Citibank was in business for more than one hundred years before its deposits reached the one-billion-dollar level.

It took a crisis to change that interest regulation because the small banks and S&Ls have about eight times more political clout than the big banks. In Cut Bluff, Montana, the president of the local bank, or S&L, is the finance chairman for the local congressman, and this is the situation all over the country —in fact, all over the world, wherever there is a multiparty political system.

If you sat up nights designing a system the consumer did not want, you would come up with something very close to today's American banking system. It wasn't intended that way. The Banking Act of 1933, commonly called the Glass-Steagall Act, provided the basic blueprint for American banking during the past fifty years. Its architects were Representative Henry Steagall, of Alabama, a member of the farm bloc, and Senator Carter Glass, a distinguished Virginian, onetime Secretary of the Treasury and the father of the Federal Reserve system. Both were fiscal conservatives and believers in competition. The senator, for example, once wrote:

> There is entirely too much running to Washington by business, by agriculture and by labor. That way lies paternalism, with socialism just beyond. There are certain things necessary to be done, of course, which the people in their private capacities lack the power to do, and in such cases the public must operate through the government . . . and it is the proper function of government to prevent the erection of any unnatural barriers to the equality of opportunity.

The Glass-Steagall Act was never intended to separate or insulate certain industries from competition. Some of the restrictions it placed on banks did protect others from competition, but this result was an incidental side effect. Its primary purpose was to protect bank depositors and stimulate business in the wake of thousands of bank failures and the revelation of shocking, criminal conflicts of interest during the go-go boom of the late 1920s. Glass-Steagall was a response to widespread losses by depositors, who are not supposed to be risk-takers, and by shareholders, who are supposed to take risks but not the risk of dishonest management.

Consequently, the Banking Act of 1933 sought to restore the solvency and strength of banks and the confidence of depositors, and it had nothing whatsoever to do with the division of markets. That was set forth clearly in its title: "An Act to provide for the safer and more effective use of the assets of banks, to regulate interbank control, to prevent undue diversion of funds into speculative operations, and for other purposes."

This legislation went about accomplishing its purpose in a number of ways. It created the Federal Deposit Insurance Corporation. It banned payment of interest on checking accounts, with the apparent purpose of using the money thus saved to pay the insurance premiums of the FDIC. It placed limitations on loans to inside executives or affiliated companies. It increased reporting and examination requirements. It prohibited risking depositors' funds in underwriting corporate securities and in related activities. It dealt with other matters affecting banks—all with the objective of protecting their solvency and their depositors' and shareholders' funds.

Another cornerstone of bank regulation, the McFadden Act, was intended to preserve our illogical dual banking system, in which some banks are chartered by the federal government and others by the states. McFadden did this by limiting deposit-taking to one state, or even just one area of that state, at the discretion of the state's authorities. In practice, it became sort of a financial Mann Act, making it illegal and immoral to transport a deposit dollar over state borders.

Stocks and other segments of the securities industry were dealt with in a different framework when Congress enacted the federal securities laws in 1933 and in 1934.

The United States has a tradition of free enterprise and competition that is not only historic but also widely regarded as the foundation of our national strength and well-being. The concept is firmly rooted both in our tradition and in our body of law: the Sherman Act, the Clayton Act, the Federal Trade Commission Act, the Robinson-Patman Act, and hosts of state laws, all reaffirming the principle of competition. Banking is the only industry that is exempted from the Clayton and the Sherman acts by the fact that it's illegal to operate across state lines.

The American principle, which has been tested and proved, is that competition most efficiently produces the greatest well-being for the greatest number of people. It is confirmed by the strength of our economic performance domestically and in the world.

But instead of a free market, the U.S. is saddled with an outmoded, anticompetitive banking system that is the most fragmented in the world. There isn't a single bank in this country that has as much as 5 percent of a market. In fact, the largest single market share was 4.3 percent, which, incidentally, was held by the ill-fated Continental Illinois Bank in Chicago. I don't know of any other major industry that fragmented.

In addition, there are 340 foreign banking offices in the U.S., which hold more than 12 percent, or almost forty billion dollars, of all loans made in this country. In New York City alone, we have ninety-odd foreign banks and they have about 40 percent of our local business. Not surprisingly, the market share of the ten largest U.S. banks has not grown in the last nine years. I don't say that with any particular pride, but nine years ago the market share of the ten largest U.S. banks was 29.8 percent and at the end of 1981 it was 27.7 percent.

Globally, we have fallen behind too. Thirty years ago, forty-four U.S. banks ranked among the world's top one hundred, with 53 percent of those banks' global deposits. By 1981, only fourteen U.S. banks were among the top one hundred, and their share of deposits had declined to 15 percent. Only two American banks now remain among the world's top ten, in contrast to twenty years ago, when U.S. banks were numbers one through ten on the list. Another number that might interest you: there are now more Japanese banks in the top fifty financial institutions of the world than there are U.S. banks—sixteen versus seven.

I don't say any of these things to decry the growth of the foreign competition or the decline of the American share. Quite the contrary, I believe that welcoming all competition has been salutary for banking in general and the customer especially.

My view, from day one, has been that instead of putting handcuffs on them, why not take the cuffs off us? I'm not afraid to compete anywhere or anytime on some kind of reasonable basis. But the competitive disadvantage for American banks has been great. A lot of the overseas banks are owned by the government, like the big French banks. They operate with thin ratios and capital bases that would put any American bank in bankruptcy. They price loans with such small markups over their own costs that their earnings are a joke.

Second, they have the support of their governments. I called around this world for over thirty-five years, and when I went abroad, a guy would say to me, "The American ambassador hasn't been to see me." And I'd reply, "Why should he?"

Then he told me that the German ambassador was just in and complained that the Deutschebank got only a little business from him last year. Why wasn't the American ambassador out selling my bank?

The last place you go to get business for an American bank is the American embassy, because we have a sort of adversarial relationship with our government.

Another advantage foreign banks have is that they were not subject to the McFadden Act's geographic restraints, which limit U.S. banks to one state only. Consequently, forty-two foreign banks operate in three or more states. The British-owned Barclays Bank has a chain of commercial bank branches in California, and banks in New York, and a commercial bank in Chicago and another in Houston. That's legal for them, but an American bank couldn't do it. When a bank was failing in Philadelphia, Mellon Bank of Pittsburgh couldn't buy it but an Arab bank did. When a big bank was failing in New York, the California-based Bank of America couldn't buy it but it was all right to sell it to the Hong Kong and Shanghai Bank, hardly a small institution on the global scene. Sumitomo, Lloyds, Banco do Brasil, Mitsubishi, Dresdner, Credito Italiano, and the Bank of Tokyo, some of the world's largest banks, are among the forty-five foreign banks that own banks in California. In fact, seven of the eleven largest banks in California are foreign-owned or -controlled. It's sort of ridiculous that they have geographic spread denied the natives.

This is not in any way to argue in favor of bigness. Big is a relative term. When I made my first airline loan, it was for a DC-3, which cost $125,000. I could have financed more DC-3s on the legal limit of Citibank then than I can finance 747s now at $85 million dollars apiece. It's a big world, and it requires big institutions to handle big problems. The factor more important than size is whether or not the system is competitive.

The word "competitive" runs through the financial services wonderland like the Mad Hatter because it seems to have a different meaning to everyone who uses it—and worse, often means different things at different times to the same people. It's what Humpty-Dumpty called a portmanteau word.

Competition, lauded as the foundation of America's strength and wealth, is a motherhood issue in theory but an abandoned child in practice. We keep looking for it, but nobody seems to know whether we are supposed to encourage it or stamp it out. The poor banker usually finds himself like Alice asking the Cheshire Cat, "Would you tell me, please, which way I ought to go from here?" and confessing she doesn't much care where she wants to get. And the grinning cat replies, "Then it doesn't matter which way you go."

That's about where we are today: trying to identify where we want to go; where we want our country to go; and how to get there. That's not easy in wonderland. But I like to think, to extend the analogy, that we are not unlike Alice and her companion, knocking on a door in Wonderland. "There's no sort of use in knocking . . ." the footman told Alice, "because I'm on the same side of the door as you are. . . . There might be some sense in your knocking if we had the door between us." One reason it is so hard to tell one side of the door from the other is that yesterday's image of the financial services business bears little relationship to today's reality. The old image is that banks are places to deposit money and get loans; that brokerage firms are places where securities are bought, sold, and distributed; that thrifts are places to maintain savings accounts and get mortgages.

Today, in financial services, you can't tell the players even with a scorecard, but that is not your fault.

Commercial banks take demand deposits and pay customers' checks drawn against them. So do credit unions, savings and loans, stockbroker cash management accounts, and money market mutual funds.

Commercial banks take time and savings deposits, and pay interest on them. So do brokers, money market funds, and all the savings and loan associations.

Commercial banks lend money secured by collateral. So do brokerage firms, leasing companies, factoring companies, captive finance companies, and aircraft engine manufacturers.

Commercial banks lend money to businesses without collateral. Businesses do too—they lend more than one hundred billion dollars to each other in the commercial paper market.

Commercial banks make personal loans and offer credit cards. So does everybody else, from finance companies to department store chains. In fact, bank-issued credit cards in the United States account for only about 15 percent of the credit card market.

Commercial banks deal in government paper. So do corporate treasurers, brokers, mutual funds, and the man in the street.

It's doubtful if there is any traditional banking service that somebody else is not also providing—and doing it nationwide.

That is what's happening in the real world. But in the *Alice in Wonderland* world of Glass-Steagall, McFadden, and protected special interests, banks still need ten messenger boys to send money across the street—one messenger boy for mortgages, another for stocks, another for installment loans, and so on, while money moves around the world at the speed of light and enters through the back door before the fastest messenger boy even steps into the street.

The reality is that the financial marketplace today is everywhere, anytime. A man in Texas takes his money out of a savings and loan and calls a toll-free telephone number in Arizona, and his money ends up in a money market fund in Boston—or anywhere else on the globe.

Financial transactions are now being performed in living rooms via cable TV or through a terminal in a corporate treasurer's office. In this kind of world, electrons have become money, credit, securities, or savings, and are more real than nineteenth-century banking palaces. The advent of electronic funds transfer and storage is as significant to the financial system today as was the substitution of paper money for gold or silver, and it has created just as big a revolution. That's what the commercial banks of America discovered when they woke up one morning and found they faced a serious competitive challenge from sources which they did not at one time regard as being in competition with banking at all. Almost every major company had a financial services division—department stores, telephone companies, broadcasting networks, engineering and construction firms, transportation operators, steelmakers, brokerage houses, and movie chains, to cite a few examples.

Sears Roebuck, for example, operates the largest savings and loan holding company in the world and its financial services operations alone earn over two hundred million dollars a year. Together with J. C. Penney and Marcor, Sears has consumer installment loans outstanding equal to roughly 12 percent of the total consumer installment debt held by *all* the commercial banks in the United States. Many of these non-bank corporations started with a captive finance subsidiary to enhance the sales efforts of the parent company. While this was the primary goal for most, some of these corporations have become highly venturesome and are now selling a vast array of financial products. Today, for example, the nation's three largest retailing chains offer everything from corporate venture capital investing and mortgage banking to consumer finance and insurance underwriting.

These retailers are an especially potent force in the consumer credit market. The credit program of Sears Roebuck alone is more sizable than either of the two national bank charge card systems. In fact, Sears with roughly twenty-five million credit cards accounted for 35 percent of the total amount owed on all U.S. bank credit cards. The success of Sears, of course, stems in no small measure from the fact that all you need anywhere in the U.S. is a shopping center and a showroom. Then you can have a mutual fund, an insurance desk, a tax expert, a travel agent, a leasing department, a real estate office, and a venture capital business right there among the refrigerators, tractors, and chain saws. American banks, which must get prior approval for every deep breath they take, are a long way from being able to compete with this "one-stop shop" concept.

In addition to the retailers, however, there are the major manufacturers of consumer durables like General Motors, Ford, and General Electric in the financial services market. These three manufacturers in combination with the three top retailers—Sears, Penney, and Marcor—hold over *four* times the national market share of the *three* largest banks in consumer credit.

Companies like ITT, Control Data, and Gulf & Western, for example, each received a third or more of their earnings from their financial operations. Borg Warner, Westinghouse, and dozens of other nonbank firms of considerable size are involved in some form of commercial finance, consumer finance, real estate, insurance, leasing, or investment services.

National Steel owns the biggest coast-to-coast federal savings and loan in the country—First Nationwide Savings. Lowes, the theater chain, also sells insurance, provides installment credit and invests in real estate. Paramount, another moviemaker, is part of the Gulf & Western conglomerate along with a bank and insurance, real estate, and mortgage companies. Texaco, best known as an oil company, formed Ful-Tex Euro services to broker time deposits, money market instruments, and foreign exchange. American Can bought Associated Madison, a billion-dollar-a-year insurance company that sells through mail order.

American Express, best known for its travel and entertainment card, also owns a cable television company, an insurance company, and a commercial bank overseas. Then it acquired Shearson Loeb Rhodes, the second-largest securities brokerage house on Wall Street. Bache, another large Wall Street house, was acquired by Prudential Insurance. Merrill Lynch, which led the Wall Street invasion into across-the-board financial services, in one way or another does everything a bank does by one name or another. Its Cash Management Account, a money market fund with check-writing privileges tied to a brokerage margin account and a high-limit credit card, set the pattern that other financial conglomerates quickly copied.

The attraction of financial services is simple. Willie Sutton, the famous bank robber, understood it clearly—that's where the money is. American consumers spend about $180 billion a year on retail financial services. An affluent household relies on an average of twenty financial vendors to purchase thirty-eight products. Less affluent families buy about twenty products from twelve sources.

U.S. banks face a considerable challenge from these competitors who are outside the banking industry. They are beating us at our own game simply because they enjoy competitive advantages on several fronts. First and foremost, there is ease of market entry—a privilege that a bank holding company does not enjoy. When both a nonbank company and a bank holding company seek to acquire a financial service operation, for example, it is to the seller's advantage to deal with the nonfinancial, and thus avoid wasting time and effort waiting around for federal approval.

When they take on a major acquisition that might violate antitrust laws, the burden of proof rests with the Justice Department and the Federal Trade Commission, which act only after the fact, if warranted. This relative freedom is in great contrast to the strict regulatory environment surrounding bank holding companies. Banks must obtain prior approval for most diversification, whether it is starting from scratch or through acquisition. In addition, the burden of proof lies with banks when it comes to showing how proposed action will serve the public benefit—a cloudy area at best, open to broad interpretation and conjecture.

Nonfinancials have a considerable competitive advantage too, in their freedom to design their capital structures, subject only to constraints imposed by financial markets. The capitalization of individual financial subsidiaries may be regulated by the various state authorities, but the parent company's capital decisions are seldom influenced by either state or federal regulators.

There is no such freedom for bank holding companies and their subsidiary banks. They must comply with the Federal Reserve standard of capital adequacy designed to protect banks from exaggerated—rather than reasonable—risks. To the extent that the Fed's standard differs from the standard considered appropriate by management, this standard may seriously restrict flexibility. Certainly, the Fed's static concept of capital adequacy, defined in ratio analysis terms, undermines the decision-making powers of management. It also ignores the changing competitive picture and the role of earnings.

We all know that risk-taking and profit-making in our society are as basic to banking as to any other business. Banks must offer services on a quality- and price-competitive basis. They must acquire capital at least cost, on prevailing risk/reward terms, and they must employ this capital in the most productive, innovative, and responsible ways they can devise. Bankers must continually develop and train new people and reset internal controls to hold down costs. This task requires sophisticated management techniques and high levels of competence which no amount of regulation can guarantee.

Voltaire once remarked that "a multitude of laws in a country is like a great number of physicians, a sign of weakness and malady." Certainly, a multitude of laws and restrictions has not contributed to the health of the American banking system.

This isn't a conspiracy, because there's nothing unusual about such events. While nonbanking competitors are free to do as they please, Congress regularly is beseeched to ban bankers from selling credit-related insurance or any number of other clearly financial-related activities, while allowing others to nibble away at bank markets.

While the public tries to get the best financial deal it can—

as it should—we have the sorry spectacle of bankers, insurance agents, securities dealers, and data-processing firms fighting each other in Washington and in the courts to protect their little monopolies.

Revenue bonds are a case in point. They barely existed in the 1930s, and in fact, the Glass-Steagall Act never mentioned them. Today, however, they account for more than 70 percent of all long-term funds raised by state and local governments. General obligation bonds, which banks are permitted to underwrite, typically sell at prices lower than revenue bonds, and the reason is obvious—more people are scrambling for the same business. When banks are kept out of the revenue bond market, the public is hurt because borrowing costs for local governments are higher, and those who aspire to keep them out are hurting the entire financial community.

Too many of us, unfortunately, practice doublethink. We defend free markets in public, but in our own offices and before government agencies we do our absolute best to create protected industries. This not only damages the fabric of the whole business community but inevitably leads to the loss of freedom. It may be obvious, but it needs repeating: protected markets are the exact opposite of free markets.

The philosophy of the divine right of kings died hundreds of years ago but not, it seems, the divine right of inherited markets. Some people still believe there's a "divine" dispensation that their markets are theirs—and no one else's—now and forevermore. It is an old dream that dies hard, yet no business person in a free society can control a market when the customers decide to go somewhere else. All the king's horses and all the king's men are helpless in the face of a better product.

Our commercial history is filled with examples of companies that failed to change with a changing world, and became tombstones in the corporate graveyard.

Investors in canal bonds in the nineteenth century who refused to invest in railroad bonds reflect the kind of vision I'm talking about. Besides saying the usual things—there're too many moving parts, I'll wait until all the technical problems are solved, it'll always be too expensive to catch on—some came up with an answer they thought irrefutable. "Railroads rust," they said, "but what can happen to a canal?" The railroads showed them, then replayed the canal scenario themselves as buses, cars, and trucks whizzed down six-lane highways and jumbo jets flew overhead while railway tracks rusted and weeds clogged what was left of the few remaining canals.

It is fair to say that the financial services business is not immune from the ancient practice of running to the government for help, but I would point to the railroads and canals and remind the safe-market seekers that there is no social security for companies in the world marketplace, no seniority rights, no disability pensions. The public doesn't really care about the internecine problems of the financial services business, nor should it. The computer and the electronic revolution have created a new marketplace and the public wants the best return on its money that these technologies can now provide, which it is entitled to. Those who seek survival in wonderland will in time discover that all the Glasses, all the Steagalls, and all the McFaddens cannot lead them back through the mirror into yesterday.

Someone might reasonably ask how commercial banks have survived this long, if the threat over the last fifty years has been that bad. One answer is that many did not. In the 1920s there were about thirty thousand commercial banks; today there are about less than half that number.

Those that remain are steadily losing their share of market. In 1946, the banking industry had a 57 percent share of American financial assets; last year it had shrunk to about 37 percent—and it is still shrinking. Between the end of 1945 and 1960, certainly a time everyone remembers as highly prosperous, the assets of commercial banks rose by three-fifths, while the asets of life insurance companies tripled, those of savings and loan associations multiplied by nine, and trusteed pension funds multiplied by fifteen.

The financial services industry is no exception to the realities of a free and open marketplace. It makes no sense to suppose that competitors would wither away under the challenge of comparably empowered banks. On the contrary, history supports the view that any industry kept in a segregated and protected market will lose its vigor but benefit from fresh competition. Separate but equal is an economic myth, as well as a social one.

All of the foregoing seems clear and straightforward. But fifty years of revisionist interpretation by determined protectionists has so muddied the picture that only the works of Professor Dodgson come close to realistically portraying the situation in financial services: "Alice thought the whole thing very absurd, but they all looked so grave that she did not dare to laugh; . . . she simply bowed . . . looking as solemn as she could."

It gets, as Alice said, curiouser and curiouser.

In 1980, for instance, Congress passed the Depository Institutions Deregulation and Monetary Control Act. After the prima facie curiosity of juxtaposing the words "deregulation" and "control" in the title, the next step was putting the job of dismantling regulation in the hands of a committee of lifelong regulators. Not surprisingly, their first step toward eliminating regulation was to establish a slate of new regulations, adding to instead of reducing the problem.

They relaxed Reg Q reluctantly, fraction by fraction, fully intending to take until 1986, which the law set as a deadline, to finish the task. But the market forced their hand. Interest rates reached 20 percent in 1982, deposits at 5.25 hemorrhaged out of the S&Ls, and to save the thrift industry the regulators had to allow banks and the thrifts to compete equally with all comers.

That episode demonstrated anew a simple fact that is unfortunately little understood.

The reason that the banking system must be competitive is that it is a *business*. The fact is that bankers are in the business of managing risk. Pure and simple, that is the business of banking. As long as a bank keeps its risks within its risk-taking capabilities, it survives; and if it doesn't, it dies. So the critical factor is the ability of a bank to earn enough to absorb its losses. No bank with strong earnings ever got into trouble. Almost all banks that have failed had adequate capital but poor earnings. The market knows the difference between strength and weakness, and its judgment is swift and harsh, as witness the Continental Illinois episode.

Another basic fact about the banking business that is little understood is that on average 70 percent of a bank's profits go back into the business. This is just the opposite of the pay-out ratio in other industries, where the stockholders get 70 percent or more of the earnings in the form of dividends. It is those profits going back into the capital base of banks that give them the capacity to finance a growing national economy. A textbook could be filled on this relationship between bank profit and economic growth. But to the man on the street it can be summed up in one four-letter word. Jobs. Everyone, in that sense, has a vested interest in maintaining a healthy banking system, because the credit-extension and money-creation function of the commercial banking system is an integral part of the job-generating economic machine, which is one reason the banking industry is the most heavily regulated in the country. My quarrel is not with regulation, as such, but with the perversion of regulation to narrow ends, which works against the public interest. Whose market is being protected from whom is not a valid question, but we all should ask: What public principles should govern our society insofar as financial markets are concerned? How will the public be best served?

Surely, all can agree on broad public policy objectives, such as: Our national policy should be to promote maximum efficiency in the capital markets; to enable and encourage financial institutions to meet the rapidly changing demands of our economy; to foster public trust in financial institutions; to encourage widespread direct public ownership of American industry; to promote fair competition; to limit the economic and political power of any one sector; and to protect investors and depositors against improper practices.

In the real marketplace, the public couldn't care less about old-fashioned and artificial distinctions. They want the best deal they can get for whatever financial service they need, and J. C. Penny, wishing to survive, gives it to them. It is not my wish to restrict the ability of Prudential-Bache, or Shearson–American Express, or any other competitor to provide quality customer services. My concern is that commercial banks are not free to compete *on equal terms* in the financial services marketplace out of a misguided fear that they would dominate it.

No one is worried that Sears Roebuck—with almost twenty-five million active credit card customers—will end retail merchandising competition. The facts of a fiercely competitive retail industry do not support that fear.

No one is afraid that Merrill Lynch—the largest brokerage house by far, with two million active customers and a branch office within twenty-five miles of three-fourths of the U.S. population—will gobble up its competitors and control everyone's financial assets.

Certainly, customers do not care who wins this obscure financial battle, because they are in the process of becoming somebody else's customers. In this age of consumerism, the public will go wherever goods and services are conveniently provided at a fair price. There is nothing wrong with this; that is what a market economy is all about. Banks cannot be sheltered from these market realities, but they are banned from participating fully and fairly in them. If banks cannot participate, they are finished as financial institutions. Those banks with no desire to become another tombstone in America's corporate graveyard may have to give up banking charters, if we want to survive into the twenty-first century.

The loss of traditional market share in the past points up an obvious truth: Whenever a business cannot or does not respond to the expressed demand of the public, a competitor moves in to fill the void. We all saw this happen when the truckers rose up to compete with the railroads, when the charter carriers made inroads into the markets of the scheduled airlines, and most recently, when cablevision began to menace television broadcasters.

What all this teaches is that competition is not a one-to-one proposition but rather a subtle evolutionary process. Those who look ahead will undoubtedly find many surprises down the road. Foresight, however, like the prophecies of Cassandra, is of little value if one lacks the flexibility to move out and meet each new challenge on an even footing.

There have been periods in our past—and not so very long ago—when political campaigners ritually looked to the time when the western farmer, the small-town businessman, and the small investor might have the same access to money and credit as a Hamilton or a Biddle or a Morgan. That time is now here. The technological conditions for fulfilling those promises exist.

Whatever the new shape of the future, one essential fact about money will not change. Gertrude Stein put it best, I think:

The money is always there, but the pockets change; it is not in the same pockets after a change; and that is all there is to say about money.

The Ultimate Loophole:
Spend Your Own Money

■ ■ ■

Anyone who has observed with sorrow the disappearance of the American handyman has had to learn some of his skills or watch the mechanical devices at home break down. In acquiring the requisite skills, one learns that a badly designed machine can never be fixed, even by an expert at tinkering. Something more radical is required—redesign.

This principle applies also to many patchwork legislative solutions to social and economic problems which have been pasted together over the years. It is the ultimate insult to say something looks as if it were designed by a committee, but to the extent we can use the word "designed," our tax laws fit that description. They were patched together by a multitude of committees over many years. All too often, changes were made without reference to what existed before. Since the beginning of time, no tax structure has ever won the plaudits of citizens. But there are few instances in history where all shades of political opinion have agreed unanimously that our tax laws are unfair, unclear and, indeed, beyond understanding. It is literally true that no one in the country knows for sure what our tax laws mean. And there is no policeman to read your rights to you if you run afoul of those laws.

It is a maxim of cryptology that what one man can devise, another can unravel. This principle keeps armies of tax lawyers and accountants employed, but adds nothing to our national productivity. The distortions in our society caused by the quirks of the law beggar the imagination. Companies that have lost money may be more valuable than others which make money. People with equal incomes pay unequal taxes. Often the heaviest burden falls on the working man or woman.

The blue-collar worker who has struggled hard to support his family, educate his children, and save his money suffers. This is the only group in our society that gets a plethora of kind words from Congress but laws that catch it in a double bind. Inflation pushes the blue-collar worker into higher tax brackets while cutting deep into his purchasing power. Savings melt under the heat of inflation, while the interest on his proposed mortgage rises beyond reach. Meanwhile, Congress increases the payments to the nonworker so that subsidies to the idle rise to meet the shrinking rewards of thrift and industry.

The issue is one of substance, rather than rates. We can fairly charge, as did our forebears in the Declaration of Independence, that taxes are "imposed without our consent." Again, we have taxation without representation because it is impossible to have your point of view fairly represented in a matter so complex that no one understands it. This lack of understanding is not limited to the ordinary person trying to pay his tax in accordance with what someone tells him the law requires. It is a pervasive malaise extending to our representatives in Congress who vote the laws in the first place. At a closed hearing on a tax bill once, several senators complained that they did not understand what they were being asked to approve. The chairman of the Senate Finance Committee is reported to have replied: "If every man insists on knowing what he's voting for before he votes, we're not going to get a bill reported out by Monday." Monday clearly had priority over clarity.

The Constitution says that Congress is to provide for the

"general welfare." Instead, Congress pays more attention to special interests. Hundreds of bills are regularly introduced to amend some part of the tax code. Many of the bills seek to benefit a sector of our society which has persuaded a congressman that it needs help. Change is then effected by amending a section of the law, often referring to another section which itself refers to still another. A recent "simple" amendment to the tax reduction bill was "read by title." The title consisted of one sentence containing sixty-nine words. Nestled among them was a key phrase, "and for other purposes." That turned out to mean anything Congress chose to put in its "Easter basket"—a plethora of tax breaks for special interests.

No congressman, no lawyer, no accountant can tell the taxpayer his rights with any certainty. No one even bothers to try to make a case that the present laws are equitable. Any law that cannot be understood is, by definition, an assault on democracy. Whenever a legislator hard-pressed for a headline needs a little free publicity, he or she announces in a tone of outrage one or another of the legitimate consequences of the law. The results are often so bizarre that each new announcement merely reinforces the public awareness that the Congress has legislated a rip-off.

One of the hallowed rites of spring used to be a legislator peering earnestly out of the television screen and bewailing the fact that some people paid no income tax. What they said was true. At one point, according to the Internal Revenue Service, there were one hundred and seven people in the United States with incomes in excess of a million dollars who paid no federal income tax. Yet no one can assert that they did not obey the law. They did no more than their Congress mandated. Obviously, such a result made no sense. No one should go tax-free. The fault, however, was not with those who paid no taxes, but with those who turned taxation into a puzzle. You can be sure that some IRS officer built a government career auditing the returns of those nontaxpayers. A law that produced this result was obviously wrong, and a minimum tax was established, though other inequities in the tax laws were left uncorrected and new ones added year by year.

Since no one believes the present laws are fair either, it is worthwhile to inquire how we got into this mess. The economist Adam Smith laid down some basic principles. Taxes should be "certain, and not arbitrary . . . clear and plain to the contributor, and to every other person." Today, taxes are uncertain, arbitrary, and unclear. Common sense has been stood on its head. We have arrived at our present absurd position because the original purposes of taxes as defined by Article One of the Constitution have been forgotten or ignored. The Constitution gave power to Congress "to lay and collect taxes" in order "to pay the debts and provide for the common defense and general welfare."

In the Constitution, no mention is made in any form of what has come to be called social engineering, a far different thing from the original idea, which was to raise money to pay the costs of government. It was a straightforward concept. Limiting taxes as a safeguard for individual liberty was much in the minds of the Founding Fathers. They knew that the power to tax was the power to destroy. They understood with great clarity that when the government takes a part of our income, it is commandeering the fruits of our labor.

As early as 1753, Benjamin Franklin suggested a standard. He wrote: "It would be thought a hard government that should tax its people one-tenth of their time, to be employed in its service." The fundamental principle laid down by our Founding Fathers has now been reversed. Today, the part of your income you succeed in keeping for yourselves is denounced as a "loophole." The ultimate logic of that assumption is that everything you earn belongs to the state. The benevolent Congress may permit you to keep a little, not as a right but only as a benefit.

Levying taxes to pay the government's bills is a sound idea. From the very start of our country, however, our toleration of taxes always has been tempered by a well-founded public awareness that government expenditures tend to be too high and to keep rising. When Thomas Jefferson won election as

President in 1800, his campaign promise was to roll back taxes. George Washington was portrayed as a big spender since he had a federal budget of about 2 percent of the national income. The budget was then financed without income taxes. The well-to-do paid a tax on imported goods, but taxation in America remained light until an income tax was levied to help finance the Civil War. That income tax was repealed in 1872. The Supreme Court found the income tax of 1894 unconstitutional.

It took a constitutional amendment in 1913 to bring the income tax back into being. Even so, as late as 1935, only one of sixty citizens was required to pay any income tax at all. To bear the cost of the New Deal and of the Second World War, one out of every three—or just about every working adult—began turning a portion of his income over to the government by the early 1940s.

No one has to remind you that federal, state, and local taxes now take more than a third of the money Americans earn. While the proportion is large and growing, the point I want to emphasize is that the tax burden does not fall upon people with any semblance of equity. The principal reason is that tax laws have not been used primarily to raise revenue. Rather, the purpose was to allocate private resources to achieve what were deemed at the time to be social priorities.

Tax policy aimed at social engineering, instead of raising revenue, inevitably provided individuals and organizations with a patchwork of deductions, exemptions, credits, and variable rates of such complexity as to boggle the mind. In moving along this path, Congress stretched the Constitution, which speaks only of the "general welfare." Far from looking to the general welfare, the tax laws help develop special interests and privileges. Doubtless, at the time they were enacted into law, each seemed like a good idea.

But our value systems constantly change. What was once thought to be good is now denounced as bad. The result is that today's social priorities will inevitably become tomorrow's tax loopholes. Examples abound: The oil depletion allowance was designed to induce people to engage in the financially risky search for petroleum because America needed supplies of energy. When Congress adopted a concurrent resolution in 1945 to allow a deduction for intangible drilling and development costs, the resolution was introduced with the words: "That in the public interest Congress hereby declares . . ." The Arab oil price increase blanked out congressional memories and turned on a spate of oratory which denounced profits as "obscene" and depletion as a "loophole." The list of special cases includes just about every category of business, labor, or voluntary organization and grows longer with every legislative tinkering. But the point is simple: When the unpleasant job of raising revenue is superseded by government allocation of resources through subsidies, exemptions, loopholes, and deductions, we end up with tax laws that are incomprehensible, and with good reason are perceived to be unfair to every sector of our society.

When a democratic consensus believes something is wrong, it is time for reform. Laws that are not only unfair but unintelligible should be repealed before social damage becomes irreparable.

The size of the IRS manual has grown to an incredible forty thousand pages. Clearly, we have arrived at the point where the tax machine has been so badly designed that no amount of tinkering can help. It is time to throw the machine away and return to the people the decision on how they wish to spend their own money.

Just as no-fault auto insurance, despite its deficiencies, leveled premiums for motorists and cut down on endless litigation in the courts, a no-fault tax policy would restore taxation to its original constitutional purpose of raising revenue and providing for the general welfare. There is much to be said for abolishing the whole complex of laws we now have and replacing it with a simple, graduated rate with no deductions, except for taxes paid to other political jurisdictions to avoid paying taxes on taxes. The exact rate is not as important as the fact that it would make the law clear, certain, and fair. It would eliminate loopholes that now make tax laws resemble a sieve and have turned tax defiance into a national pastime.

Since only people pay taxes, the present policy of differentiating between corporate and personal income taxes makes absolutely no sense. In reality, corporate and personal taxes are one and the same. A large percentage of the population has a stake in corporations by either owning shares directly or owning life insurance and pension funds that make the investments. In fact, the greatest asset the workingman has is a future claim on his pension. Directly or indirectly, the retired worker must rely on corporate payments for his pension. The majority of jobs in this country are provided by corporations. Whether or not one works for a corporation, everyone is a consumer, and in the end the consumers pay the corporate tax. If the tax is too high, the buyer pays more for the product of the corporation. If the buyer refrains from buying, then shareholders' dividends decline or evaporate and the workingman's paycheck shrinks or disappears. Since it is a truism that no country can be richer than what it can produce, income can be divided but not multiplied through tax laws.

If the tax rate were the same for corporations and individuals, the shareholder and the workingman would have more money to spend, not as the government decides but as they choose for themselves. Free people, making free choices in a free marketplace, form the wellspring of our economy. Business would be spurred to research, investment, and development. As a consequence, it would hire, compete, and produce more and more at less and less cost. This program would answer the fears of a capital shortage, because capital is nothing more than stored-up labor. To the extent that all people can keep more of the fruits of their labors, more capital is available to increase production and the quality of life.

This simple but fundamental truth has not been observed by those who determine our tax policy. Voted in response to populist pressure to tap the corporate exchequer, negative sanctions on saving and investment have depleted the public's pocketbook, thrown people out of work, and weakened the economy.

The cold fact is that the Congress, business, labor, and individuals have a vested interest in the complexity of the tax laws. The beneficiaries of tax breaks regard them as constitutional rights. Their proponents in the Congress use them as a means to court their constituents and ensure reelection. Out of habit, the homeowner thinks his deduction for mortgage interest is all that stands between him and foreclosure. The biggest subsidy of all goes to the people who live in suburban houses. They get a six-billion-dollar marker for interest on their mortgages. Those of us who live in apartments feel that is not equitable. The businessman insists that the investment tax credit is the only thing that stands between progress and stagnation. I think, for example, the bad-debt deduction is one of the finest ideas in the history of the world. That's *my* loophole. But of course, *your* loophole is very unjust. Doctors and lawyers, farmers and laborers, young and old, rich and poor, all have been seduced by the psychology of entitlement. They have become habituated to look to government to subsidize, directly or indirectly, their education, their homes, their food, their medical care, and their retirement. Each person regards the other man's loophole as evil, but his own as essential. The universities, the hospitals, and all other charitable organizations have such faith in the American people that they say nobody would give them any money if it were not a tax deduction. That just isn't so. The greatest period for giving in American history occurred before the income tax. A Carnegie Library in every town in the Midwest testifies to that. I submit that if you and I could keep 80 percent of our earnings, we'd be delighted to continue to support the universities, the hospitals, and other charitable foundations. Congress, instead of placing a tax reduction under public scrutiny, all too often prefers obscure subsidies and loopholes with complex credits, deductions, and tax carrybacks; it fills the law with these and other riddles. As long as handouts to rich and poor alike are buried in the maze of our tax structure, public confidence in the fairness of the rule of law will continue to decline.

At a time when people grow cynical about all institutions that promise more than can be delivered, it is time for reform. What is needed is a simple, clear tax law, understandable to all, to reduce bias and restore balance. It is time to recognize that freedom and incentives—not tax dodges or loopholes—are what inspire people to work, to save, and to invest. Let us return these decisions to the people by eliminating our present maze of laws and putting in a simple graduated rate unencumbered by exemptions, deductions, deferrals, loopholes, incentives, or disincentives. Perhaps then we can begin to repair the social fabric.

Freedom can be as effectively destroyed by a tax policy designed to allocate resources as it can by the repeal of the First Amendment. When business and personal decisions are not made on economic grounds, but are shaped by tax consequences, which may or may not make any economic sense, our American system of economic and political freedom is in jeopardy. The framers of the Constitution were well aware of this danger, since they were the victims of discriminatory tax acts promulgated from across the seas. Governments have not mended their ways any more than human nature has changed. Using tax policy to either force or induce people to do what the government wants, and not what the citizen exercising his free choice wants, is based on the assumption that government knows best. It reflects a distrust of freedom.

A paternal government permitting some favored section of our population to benefit more from the results of their labor than some other section illustrates a point made by the great Justice Louis Brandeis when he wrote:

> Experience should teach us to be most on our guard to protect liberty when the government's purposes are beneficent. . . . The greatest dangers to liberty lurk in insidious encroachment by men of zeal, well-meaning but without understanding.

Our tax laws are written by people of zeal, and it is equally true that they surpass all understanding.

From Adam to George, from 1776 to 1984

· ■ ·

All of us remember the old Charlie Chaplin film depicting a man caught up in a huge machine. Despite his best efforts, he became a cog in the turning wheels of the machine he was trying to fix. Those old machines are gone now, but they have been replaced by a new kind of dilemma. The mechanical machines are now electronic, and instead of running around with a wrench and an oil can, we are condemned to filling out endless forms replete with warnings of dire consequences concerning entry of false data. While this is part of modern life, I would pose two questions: First, what is it we are really trying to do? Second, does what we are now doing help us achieve the desired result?

To put those questions in context, it is necessary to recall that there are still only two basic models of human organization: the authoritarian in its many guises, and the democratic. In its simplest terms: power from the top down or the bottom up. That thread of political evolution is inextricably linked with economic theory and practice in the nations of the world.

In our political evolution, Americans drew heavily on the ideas of British thinkers, especially John Locke, and, in a sense, went even further by adopting a Constitution based on the accuracy of Lord Acton's dictum that "power corrupts and absolute power corrupts absolutely." That belief led to the explicit division of powers among our President, our Congress, and our courts.

This constitutional separation of powers gives us a few bad moments from time to time. The orderly formation of policy sometimes appears to be frustrated. Our system is untidy, it is difficult, and it is further confused by the fact that the media occasionally anoint one or another arm of our government and proclaim its ascendancy. Everyone remembers reading about the imperial President, or the primacy of the Supreme Court when President Roosevelt claimed progress was being blocked by nine old men. Most recently, Congress was accused of running five hundred and thirty-five State Departments. But with it all, the main purpose is achieved—individual liberty in America has been not only preserved but enhanced. There are few countries on earth that have enjoyed that experience.

It was more than a matter of luck. The political concepts we imported from England happily coincided with the economic ideas of Adam Smith and together they provided the basis for the remarkable growth of the American nation in the nineteenth century. By coincidence, Smith's *Inquiry into the Nature and Causes of the Wealth of Nations* was published in Scotland in the same year as our Declaration of Independence was proclaimed in Philadelphia.

The name Adam Smith is probably best known today as the pseudonym of a popular writer and television commentator on financial matters, so it is worthwhile to recall that the original Adam Smith was a somewhat eccentric Edinburgh professor of Political Economy and Moral Philosophy, as the dismal science was called in those days. Though he was apt to walk in the rain without his umbrella or start for his lecture hall not fully clothed, Adam Smith's intellect was crystal-clear. He viewed the dawn of the Industrial Age and grasped its potentials while the conventional wisdom of his era was still wedded to restrictive mercantile principles. Smith sensed, long before others, that free markets could unlock a torrent of economic expansion leading to a better life for all, in stark contrast to the static mercantilist partnership of state and business that set limits for products, production, prices, and profits and distributed the benefits to a favored few. Though a devoutly religious man, Adam Smith was a pragmatist who had few illusions about his fellow man's altruistic instincts. His opinion of businessmen was particularly realistic, to say the least:

> He generally . . . neither intends to promote the public interest, nor knows how much he is promoting it. By preferring the support of domestic to that of foreign industry, he intends only his own security; and by directing that industry in such a manner as its produce may be of the greatest value, he intends only his own gain and in this as in many other cases, is led by an invisible hand to promote an end which was no part of his intention. . . . [But] by pursuing his own interest he frequently promotes that of the society more effectively than when he really intends to promote it. I have never known much good to be done by those who affected to trade for the public good. It is an affectation, indeed, not very common among merchants, and very few words need be employed in dissuading them from it.

My friend Professor George Stigler, one of our Nobel laureates in economics, has observed that "unfortunately, in a rare display of reticence, Adam Smith failed to tell us what those few words are."

The truth is that the Father of Capitalism did not have a high opinion of capitalists. What he understood was that multitudes of human beings pursuing their own best interest will ultimately produce a sort of common denominator from which we all have a chance of getting the best available deal at the moment. This state of affairs also has a way of liberating a great deal of human energy, directing it toward finding better or cheaper ways of doing things. He also understood that the diffusion of power, both political and economic, could and would create the conditions for human freedom and economic innovation. All power, no matter how derived, either from the bottom up or the top down, can be arbitrary. Only in the multiplicity of power is there safety.

Smith's desire to keep government's hands off business had nothing to do with protecting business from government. On the contrary, it was his knowledge that whenever business and government walk hand in hand, the inevitable result is to afford some businessmen the opportunity to keep others out of the marketplace. He did not consider this to be in the interest of the consumer—or, as Smith might have said, the common man. What it gets you is higher prices and less innovation, and there are plenty of examples of that right up to our own time.

Smith didn't think much of governments' proclivities to tax, either. He noted that "there is no art which one government sooner learns of another, than that of draining money from the pockets of the people." That observation is some two hundred years old but it still has a certain validity.

The link between free markets and free men and women has been apparent to all who would look, because a directed economy must, in the end, be backed by governmental edict to function at all. Absent such force, markets will let individuals decide how to allocate their own time and money, and this will often be at variance with the central plan, or whatever euphemism for it is in vogue at a given moment.

Any central economic plan involves choices because resources, no matter how large, are still finite. Since few of these choices can be put to a majority vote, more and more are assigned to experts, who then substitute their judgment for the market. It is a poor trade. The market is the greatest data processor in existence. It adjusts for things seen and unseen in a way no single person can perceive. Its ability to sift through the mass of data and arrive at a conclusion on everything from the dollar-yen cross-rate to the price of a given product is frustrating to people who believe a particular professional discipline should have more influence on prices than it has.

The fact that the market makes judgments at variance with what you and I might regard as the "correct judgment" based on our perception of the "facts" in no way alters the reality of the efficient market.

The alternative is a world in which, as Milton Friedman has said, "whatever is not compulsory is forbidden."

In our democracy, public policy results from the complex interaction of what people think an economic and political system should be and what they believe it to be at the moment. It is the disparity between what they conceive of as the *ideal* and what they perceive as *real* that fuels the engine of social change. Both concepts, the ideal and the real, have always been influenced by the pamphleteer or his equivalent, which nowadays may range from a respected think tank to a rock composer.

The difference between then and now is that the scholarly ideas of Adam Smith or the incendiary words of Thomas Paine were read by a few hundred people, but the staged demonstration at a nuclear plant enters fifty million living rooms on the evening television news with devastating effect.

The impact of this continuous flow of fact, fiction, data, information, and misinformation has had a profound effect on American society in general and on business in particular. We have become the first human society to live in a state of what the late George Gallup called "a continuous audit."

The power of the computer has played no small role in creating this unlimited proliferation of data. Consequently, it is always possible to look back and find a piece of the data somewhere in the memory banks to prove that somebody knew something years ago and failed to act upon that information responsibly or acted in violation of some law or regulation. As long as the trail is wide and long and prolix, which the computer assures it will be, commentators, lawyers, and regulators can dig through a billion pieces of paper, or their electronic equivalents, as they did in the long-playing International Business Machines and American Telephone and Telegraph antitrust suits, until it becomes statistically inevitable that any given proposition can be *proved* after the fact.

That one item may range from the presence of a Russian brigade in Cuba that appears and reappears like the Cheshire Cat, sitting on an international limb, to a loan or an investment that goes bad, thereby proving to the critics that it should never have been made in the first place. This continuous audit cannot fail to have a significant and inhibiting effect on the way we conduct our affairs.

Just as we find it increasingly difficult to determine *when* we know something, so it is also more difficult to decide *what* we know, for the line has been blurred between random information and the reality about which we need to be informed. Indeed, it can be argued that the importance of the legal and regulatory paper trail has made the manual of procedure more important than the act itself. We resemble the line from *My Fair Lady,* when Professor Higgins says that "the French don't care what you do, actually, so long as you pronounce it properly." We have become so entranced with pronouncing it properly in our electronic data entries that we sometimes forget what it is we are trying to do. The production of statistics and reports has become an end in itself, and threatens to lead us into a new form of mercantilism in electronic disguise. Adam Smith would have no trouble in seeing where the miles of printouts lead.

It might add to our perspective a bit if we reminded ourselves where we got the word "statistics" in the first place. It was given to us by a Scottish gentleman named Sir John Sinclair, who imported it from Germany in 1791 and used it in the title of his book, *A Statistical Account of Scotland.* The German term, he tells us in his preface, did not quite describe his own purposes. Sir John was interested in "the quantum of happiness enjoyed by the inhabitants and the means of its improvement," but in Germany the word *Statistik* was confined to matters concerning the political strength of the state. A case can be made that the original German concept of statistics is now working its way into our country on the back of the technologically driven data explosion.

Underlying the whole process is, of course, the revolution that began with the first electronic computer in 1945. Every item in business today leaves an electronic trail—of research, development, design, manufacture, distribution, marketing, and accounting. We find the laws and regulations concerned more with assuring a clearly marked trail than with the final results. A single number, which appears to be finite, is itself the end result of many guesses and can be, and often is, communicated worldwide in minutes. We have reached the point where the statistics of the gross national product or the composite index of leading indicators can cause a major rally or slump on Wall Street when released. In that situation, the index is not a statistical report *about* what is happening in the world. Publication of the statistic *is* the happening, even though the number probably will be revised in a few weeks.

Governments have fared no better. There is more than a little truth in the remark of a former British Chancellor of the Exchequer that there was no balance-of-payments problem in the nineteenth century because there were no balance-of-payments statistics. In fact, nobody ever attempted to work out the statistic before the 1930s. The old-time policymakers only dimly realized that it might theoretically exist. They looked instead to the movement of gold reserves, and if that was creating a problem, it was usually something that could at least wait until after lunch.

Today, any government in the world that announces a change in its fiscal or monetary policies can find out in a matter of minutes what the world thinks of the development by watching the exchange rate on its currency, which alters almost instantly in the money markets in London, Zurich, or Tokyo. The old gold exchange standard of yesterday has been replaced by an electronic information system that can be more or less harsh than the gold standard but, in the end, is just as sure and just as certain.

The incessant production of new data and its instantaneous communication throughout the world thus creates a paradox: Information, which we have always viewed as the thing that eliminates uncertainty, now increases everybody's feeling of insecurity because of the failure to convert data into knowledge.

That feeling of insecurity, in turn, creates an insatiable demand, both in public opinion and in the halls of government, to "get things under control." If we subjected our health to the same process, we would take our blood pressure every hour. That drumbeat of data could lead us to the conclusion that we are very sick men and women when in fact we are only measuring the normal rhythm of life.

The resultant hypochondria is providing a ready market for the peddlers of miracle cures in bottles of all shapes and sizes. What they have in common is almost always a label that reads "to be taken with large doses of government intervention."

Under the banner of protecting the small investor, the Securities and Exchange Commission now requires reams of data that are so comprehensive no small investor could possibly get anything out of them. The requirement to produce these data clearly is part of an effort to control the governance of American business, rather than arising from any concern to protect the small investor.

One of my Walter Mitty dreams was to be allowed to keep the books of Citicorp the same way for two years in a row so we, and our stockholders, would know how we were doing. That never happened; each year brought mandated accounting "improvements," which supposedly had a sound conceptual base but, nevertheless, changed the numbers in greater or lesser ways, making it difficult to interpret results on a consistent basis. While consistency may be the hobgoblin of little minds, as Emerson said, it also has its uses. Disclosure, the touchstone of investor protection, became stylized like a Kabuki dance while information presented in other formats was regarded by some as offering no real protection. This point of view reached its level of *reductio ad absurdum* when a legislative committee of New York State held hearings to imply that bankers did not make full disclosure about what they knew about New York City's finances. At a hearing, I held up the front page of the New York *Daily News,* a newspaper that then had the country's largest circulation. The headline, covering the entire front page, read "City Broke." I argued—not unreasonably, I thought—that a paper read by millions of people constituted full disclosure. And yet some people, with straight faces, advanced the notion that since it was not in fine print in a prospectus, this was not true disclosure. In the end common sense prevailed, but it was a near thing. If the purpose of disclosure is to warn and inform the investing public, certainly the front page of the *Daily News* is at least as effective as a 10K. On the other hand, if the goal is not really to inform but rather to conform to a requirement for completing a form devised by lawyers in a certain way, it is inadequate. So we return to the first question I posed: What are we trying to do? It seems to me what we should be trying to do is to produce reliable, timely, informative data within an understandable framework that allows people to make informed judgments.

Clearly, we must have a set of standards if we are not to have chaos. At the same time, statisticians, accountants, and the regulators who have the power to mandate reporting rules must come to grips with the question of what information is relevant for decision-making. I would suggest that they use the old adage "Less is more" as their guide. Our ability to discern what is important and what is not may be impaired if one is inundated by a sea of numbers. Too many numbers may make the decision-making process harder, not easier.

All of life is the management of risk, not its elimination. We can have too much exercise, or too little; too much food, or too little; too much medical attention, or too little; take too much risk with our investments, or too little. Increased disclosure may help reduce ignorance-induced risk but can never protect against the natural risks inherent in decision-making. When I started out as a credit officer, I used to go down the street to a lending officer at another bank and ask him, "Is company X's credit any good?" He would say "Yes" or

"No." And that was a credit check. The assumption today is that more and more statistics make life less dangerous, but the high number of loan write-offs and bankrupt companies fail to prove the case.

Of more significance is the fact that the mere production of all these data is pushing business back to a discredited form of economic policy that has been dressed up in new fashions which appeal to some modern business managers. It was packaged most attractively by a former President of the United States, who once referred to it in a State of the Union address as a partnership between government, business, and labor.

For such a partnership to exist, we would have to adopt the view that business has become a separate class with interests independent of those of its owners and employees. We would also have to accept the proposition that the almost three million workers in the federal government are no longer the servants of the citizens, as envisioned by our Constitution, but also have become a separate estate, with interests distinguishable from those of the people they are elected or appointed to serve.

Once one swallows that premise, logic would suggest that there has been a separation of ownership and management of the American corporation. That, in turn, is used to make the argument that the corporation has a life of its own, independent of its owners and their interest. Doubt is thus cast upon the corporation's legitimacy. Data are then produced to show to the prosecutor's satisfaction that the corporate power to influence output, employment, and the income of millions of Americans is growing year by year. The historical justification for private ownership of the means of production—namely, that it would produce via the force of competition in the marketplace the highest social product—appears to have been undermined. The length of the road we have come can be measured by two incidents: first, the flap caused in 1953 when Charlie Wilson supposedly said that what was good for General Motors was good for America, and second, when the Ninety-sixth Congress bailed out the Chrysler Corporation and thereby repealed the right to fail as public policy.

Private ownership has become so subverted that the employees—including the professional managers—have become wards of the state. Indeed, the bailout of the Chrysler Corporation by the federal government, as a denial of the right of private owners to fail, logically leads to the denial of the right to succeed. If all this is accepted, it becomes clear that so-called excess earnings are now justifiably claimed by government. The chain is complete in which the government has transferred the wealth of savers and equity holders to others in our society. Since markets cannot be fooled over time, this massive income transfer is reflected in the fact that the real rate of return on the Standard and Poor common stock index has been negative since 1967.

The litany of what we have done to effect this transfer of wealth from the saver to the spender would make the old mercantilists green with envy.

It all adds up to a kind of modern mercantilism in electronic clothing that is packaged as partnership. However flattering this partnership role might seem, and it is very attractive to some businessmen, there are at least two things wrong with it. First, it contradicts the basic American principle that our society is a collection of individuals, not institutions, and that the basis of our political liberty is individual liberty. Carried to its logical conclusion, this view of society must ultimately replace the idea of the individual as the center of our society with the notion of the *Standestaat.* The second thing wrong with the partnership concept is that to the extent that it succeeds, it will be an economic disaster. It replaces economic competition among various entities with political competition. It creates an environment in which a corporation's well-being depends less and less on its ability to produce a salable product or service and more and more on its ability to secure a favorable interpretation of some obscure subparagraph in the *Federal Register.*

Corporations are the economic agents of the people just as surely as governments are their political agents. The failure to preserve this distinction between the proper roles of economic agents and political authorities threatens to politicize all economic decision-making. To the extent that occurs—and, in fact, it already has begun to occur—it will impair fundamentally the capacity of the business system to provide jobs and raise productivity. Once the economic marketplace is replaced by the political process, what Franklin Roosevelt called "the great arsenal of democracy" will be replaced by a shrinking pie with special-interest political groups fighting over their share. The state will become the receiver in bankruptcy of impotent individual responsibility.

In the short run, some corporate managers are tempted to participate in the political game to curry favor, and many have done so in the belief that the survival of their enterprises depends on it. But the longer-term result of this business-political strategy is to bring all decisions concerning output, employment, and resources allocation to Washington. Once that is achieved, one of its worst effects—resulting from a flood of regulations, laws, and publicity—is the creation of a powerful incentive to avoid risk of any kind.

The process tends to nullify the capital value of organizations designed to make economic decisions on economic grounds. Although there are undoubtedly many reasons for the significant decline in the real market value of American corporations, this phenomenon surely has to rank as one of the most important.

We have revived Colbert's ancient and disastrous system of "restraint and regulation" from the court of Louis XIV with an efficiency beyond anything he could have dreamed or imagined. Today, it is even more dangerous because we have something Colbert lacked. We have computerized data. The combination of mercantilist ideas with the torrents of information that inundate American society may be a greater threat to the survival of our system of democratic capitalism than the Great Depression or World War II.

Oliver Wendell Holmes once remarked that there are times when "we need education in the obvious more than investigation of the obscure." What needs to be made obvious today is that the solutions concocted by Colbert and Louis XIV will not work any better on the floppy disks of computers than they did in the Hall of Mirrors at Versailles.

What needs also to be made obvious is that you and I who have enjoyed that rarest of commodities, economic and political freedom, have a responsibility to preserve and protect it for our successors as our forebears did since 1776. More than two hundred years have elapsed since John Locke and Adam Smith laid the foundation for the benefits we enjoy today. Those benefits are not enshrined in a perpetual contract but rather in one that requires continual renewal. George Orwell reminded us of that necessity in his gloomy view of a future society, dominated by Big Brother, in which there was no freedom, no privacy, no individuality. He wrote:

> The party . . . sought power because men in the mass were frail, cowardly creatures who could not endure liberty or face the truth, and must be ruled over and systematically deceived by others who were stronger than themselves. That the choice for mankind lay between freedom and happiness, and that, for the great bulk of mankind, happiness was better.

As it turned out, Orwell was wrong—at least in his timing. The year 1984 came and went and although Big Brother is uncomfortably pervasive in our lives, he is being held at bay. Part of the reason the grim society Orwell predicted did not materialize is that a free economic system and political freedom go hand in hand.

Adam Smith's invisible hand still produces more for most people than the heavy authoritarian hand of George Orwell's Big Brother.

The Land Where No One
Speaks the Truth

▪ ■ ▪

Henry Wallich, who was a professor at Yale and later a governor of the Federal Reserve, likens inflation to living in a country where nobody speaks the truth. The veracity of this observation is demonstrated daily in the fears over inflation. Whenever this regressive tax rises to the point where it becomes politically intolerable, each sector of society attempts to explain the common dilemma in terms of how it affects that single sector. The housing people talk of their inability to fulfill the Great American Dream of home ownership. Labor avers that it is a victim and not the cause of the problem. Business, because of the broad horizon it spans, is both victim and villain, often simultaneously. Government blames us all. Its spokesmen travel around the country telling people that the real villains in the inflation story are businessmen who raise their prices, or labor unions that raise wages, or the media which inform about inflation, or consumers who borrow too much and save too little.

To get blamed for acts you do not commit, or for the bad news created by somebody else, is a hazard that happens to bankers, businessmen, labor leaders, and almost anyone else involved in handling money. In the business community, we are treated to an especially strong dose of this misdirected anger because the bad news is delivered in the highly visible form of rising prices. To report that the price of everything has gone up is another way of saying that the value of your money has gone down. Since only the government prints money, it does not like people being told that the value of its product is deteriorating.

It is helpful to remember, however, that rising prices or wages do not cause inflation; they only report it. They represent an essential form of economic speech, since money is just another form of information. So are prices, which enable consumers to communicate with producers and tell them what they want or don't want. If prices are censored, or frozen, they cannot tell producers what goods or services people want or don't want. Examples abound.

When the government artificially restrained prices for natural gas some years ago, the price told consumers that this form of energy was relatively cheap and in ample supply. Believing what they heard, people built houses heated with natural gas. The same controlled price told producers that people did not want natural gas—it was not in demand—and therefore they had no incentive to increase production. Everybody was being deceived and we all learned the results in the winter of 1976–1977, when there was a severe shortage of natural gas.

People are also often deceived also about the nature of money. As a piece of paper in your pocket, money has no intrinsic value. It is worthless. Its only value is in what it represents, which is a claim on a share of the world's goods and services. If the government increases the number of pieces of paper called money faster than the private sector can produce goods and services, then every piece of paper is going to represent a smaller claim on whatever people have to sell. The only way to keep that from happening is either to increase the production of something salable, or else to slow down production of the pieces of paper.

A government traditionally exercises its political control

over the economy in two major ways: it decides how much money to print, and then it decides how much of that money to take back in the form of taxes. Most of the tax money, of course, is later pumped or pushed back into the economy in the form of government spending on goods, social welfare payments, or salaries to government employees. The only time money moves with something like its own free will is during the brief interval between coming off the printing presses and being captured by the tax collector. One might think that such cradle-to-grave control would satisfy the government and give the various bureaucracies enough to keep them busy. But the way the government has handled its two main operations—printing money and taxing it—has so bollixed up the economy that it sometimes feels obliged to go further and impose more controls on what happens to our money during its brief period of freedom between printing press and tax collector.

It usually justifies this action by blaming business for raising prices and blaming labor for raising wages, and in the process also lectures consumers on their spending habits.

Adam Smith described the scenario as long as two hundred years ago:

> It is the highest impertinence and presumption . . . in kings and ministers, to pretend to watch over the economy of private people and to restrain their expense, either by sumptuary laws, or by prohibiting the importation of foreign luxuries. They are always and without exception, the greatest spendthrifts in the society. Let them look well after their own expenses and they may safely trust private people with theirs. If their own extravagance does not ruin the state, that of their subjects never will.

Governments' ability to devastate an economy and blame it on someone else should never be underestimated. They have been doing it for a long, long time, even before Adam Smith chronicles the tendency. The ancient Persian empire of Arta-xerxes II overtaxed and overspent to such an extent that economic unrest weakened it. The resultant political instability made possible its conquest by Alexander the Great in 334 B.C. The Chinese invented paper money in A.D. 970 but were forced to abandon its use by A.D. 1425 because of inflation. Governments do not even have to use paper money to get into trouble. The riches of El Dorado—the precious metals flowing into Europe from Mexico and Peru—formed the basis for an inflation that in the end destroyed the Spanish Empire. Every time a new silver consignment arrived at Seville, a ripple of price increases spread across Europe because there was suddenly more money with which to buy things. Because the effect was always felt first and strongest in Spain, that country continuously occupied top place in the inflationary table. Spanish costs became increasingly uncompetitive, and the Dutch got rich buying cheaper goods in the north and shipping them south. The Spanish solution was to sink merchant ships and hang businessmen.

You can find the same story of unsuccessful repression of economic news being repeated all the way back to the Roman emperor Diocletian, who may have coined the best name yet for government price controls: *argumentum baculinum,* or argument of the club. The penalty for violating the controls set by Diocletian on fifteen thousand commodities was death, which even John Kenneth Galbraith would say was significant.

It is, as you see, an old story. Yet each era ignores the lessons of the past and is forced to relearn the bitter truth anew.

We Americans do not have to look back to China, Spain, or Rome to find examples of economic mismanagement. We have gone through the whole sequence ourselves in the past couple of decades. In fact, reading the papers today is like watching reruns on the late late show—I know what will happen in the next reel. In the wake of the Vietnam war, we ran the gamut of *argumentum baculinum,* from jawboning to price freezing, and the only thing that finally moderated the rise in inflation was the recession of 1973–1975, the worst since the Great Depression up to that time. Because nothing was done about the underlying causes on a continuing basis, after that recession was over, prices went up again and interest rates reached a level in 1980–1981 that had not been seen since 1878. There we were again, doing it all over under a different administration and with a different party in the White House.

The plain fact is that we have had inflation in this country since 1967 because the government caused the money supply to grow nearly three times faster than the goods and services that could be bought with it. That statement can be fiddled with, statisticized, and footnoted until everybody forgets what is being talked about. But the bad news will not go away. No amount or kind of wage and price controls can make a government's paper money worth more of the world's goods and services than the world is prepared to give for them.

Despite all of the sophisticated statistics pouring out of Washington, the fact remains that the only institution that can create inflation is government itself. Inflation doesn't grow on trees. It's made by people, real live people, living in Washington, who collectively make up the government and like to keep their jobs. They respond to political pressures in a way that causes the government continuously to spend more money, and when it finds itself spending more than it is taking in, it solves the problem by printing more money. Our fiscal and monetary authorities, the Congress and the Federal Reserve Board, can always spare the country the disaster of inflation by simply avoiding the overspending and the overprinting.

Unable to control itself in these two critical areas, the government periodically decides to control everyone else. It goes after the borrowers and lenders and uses its political clout to compel them to handle their money in ways that run counter to their own self-interest. The compulsion comes with the innocuous label "credit controls" and a promise that they will cure all economic ills quickly.

This has never worked in history. One reason it never works is that when the government tries to allocate credit, it is subject to the same irresistible political pressures that make it print and spend too much money in the first place.

Let me cite just one example. Within a few hours after President Carter announced his anti-inflation program in 1979, the Federal Reserve Board put out a regulation specifying that no bank could increase its total loans and investments by more than 6 to 9 percent. It took the governors of the fifty states of the Union about thirty seconds to realize that if commercial banks were prevented from buying their state bonds as an investment under this ruling, state governments would be unable to meet their payrolls. So the telephone lines began humming between Washington and the state capitals, and within forty-eight hours that particular problem disappeared. An average citizen, looking for an emergency bank loan to help meet his April income tax payment, of course, might have been out of luck. His need may have been as great, and even the government would have to admit that he intended to put the money to good use, but he lacked the political clout.

Once the government reaches its hands into the credit markets, it is no longer enough to have a good credit rating —you must also have friends in government. The invisible handshake is the inevitable by-product of allocating credit through the political process and not through the economic process.

The second reason government credit allocation never works is that people are not stupid. The public was ripped off for decades by government regulations that prohibited banks from paying you more than 5.25 percent on savings accounts. This inequity, in combination with various state usury laws which controlled the amount of interest that could be charged on a loan or an installment purchase, merely meant that the person who worked hard and saved money subsidized all those who wished to borrow.

Learned authorities, surveying the resulting carnage of inflation, blame the consumer. One respected economist put it this way:

> At the focal point [of inflation] has been the atypical behavior of the American consumer. As inflation rose . . . the consumer, instead of maintaining his savings rate and lowering his spending, did just the opposite. He maintained his spending and lowered his savings rate. . . . Moreover . . . the consumer has been steadily substituting borrowing as a means of wealth building and maintaining living standards.

It would be hard to improve on this analysis. What is surprising is that the behavior of the American consumer should be regarded as "atypical." After all, the federal government controlled the amount customers could earn on their savings. The savings account, traditional saving tool of small savers, could not pay even a third the rate of inflation. The savings certificates used by more well-to-do savers also paid considerably less than the rate of inflation. And as if limiting these earnings wasn't enough, the government also taxed them. So a typical consumer might have earned around 3.5 percent after tax from a savings account, or 9 percent after tax from a "high-interest" savings certificate.

At the same time, price controls in the form of state usury laws set the rate that consumers paid to borrow. The government let borrowers write the interest off their income tax. A typical consumer might have paid, after tax, 9 percent for a mortgage or 12 percent for a personal loan. When inflation was at 18 percent at its high point and the prime rate over 16, these controls in the guise of regulations subsidized borrowing.

People are pretty smart. They had no trouble figuring out that if they earned 3 percent on their savings when inflation was in double digits, then the system was stealing them blind.

They also perceived that if they borrowed at 9 or 12 percent when inflation was 18, then they were beating the system.

Under these circumstances, consumers showed unimpeachable logic and common sense—they saved less and borrowed more. That experts found this behavior to be "atypical" is astonishing. What is even more astonishing is that the government, having made this the only logical course for a sensible consumer, then denounced this inevitable behavior as a major contributor to the inflation that threatened the nation.

Savings are the only true source of capital, and what we had in this country was a set of laws designed to penalize people for saving money. To say that America has the lowest savings rate of any industrialized nation is also to say that it is accumulating capital at a slower rate than anyone else. The longer this process continues, the worse our situation will become. Without capital, we cannot produce the goods and services necessary to soak up the output of the government's money presses. In the long run, we will lose our competitive position in the world because we cannot produce the new technologies and efficiencies necessary to compete with countries like Germany and Japan, where the savings rate is 13 percent and 22 percent, compared to our own paltry 3.4 percent rate.

At the same time, as a veteran of the New York City financial crisis, I am acutely aware that every line in the government's budget has a constituency. Everyone in America has by now made some kind of handshake deal with some level of government—federal, state, or municipal. Lewis Lapham, writing in *Harper's,* only mildly overstated the case when he pointed out that:

> Within its own borders the United States awards nearly 50 percent of its tax revenues as transfer payments to whatever lobbies, special interests, and racial or sexual minorities . . . hold the government hostage in

Washington. The huge sums of money listed in the budget as fundings for the purposes of health, education, welfare, and social security represent only a small part of the annual ransom paid to the more successful syndicates in the society.

So the political pressure on government to run deficits is very heavy. A government's promise to stop printing money is frequently like the alcoholic's resolution to have just one more drink.

Since the beginning of time, governments have sought simple, sugar-coated solutions. A long time ago, King Charles II instructed his Parliament: "I pray contrive any good short bills which may improve the industry of the nation."

There were no "good short bills" then, nor are there any now. All of the great issues of our time, and most of the small ones, are settled in the untidy atmosphere of give and take, negotiation and compromise.

Today, you can sell a lot of papers by saying the world is in for a replay of the tragedy of the 1930s. This scenario assumes that we have learned nothing. That is not so. All governments have become much more sophisticated in operating their monetary machinery. Most important, they have devised mechanisms of cooperation which are kept in good repair. The world has moved from the rigidity of the gold exchange standard to floating rates that now permit the system to bend without breaking. Central banks are particularly alert to their role as lenders of last resort. Various institutions for international stability, such as the International Monetary Fund and the World Bank, have grown more mature.

There is now no doubt that all governments can—if they will—curb inflation by practicing monetary and fiscal restraint and encouraging productivity. Progress in any form, however, takes time, and most bureaucracies move at a ponderous pace. Cutting the money supply, which inevitably creates some unemployment and stagnation in the economy, is often viewed as too slow and too painful a remedy to cure the virus.

Although strong medicine is needed to take the high fever out of inflation, people become restive and demand immediate relief. This impatience, of course, is understandable in a world that has grown accustomed to miraculous cures, wonder drugs, and instant answers. The danger comes when politicians in an effort to please their constituents turn from economic to political strategies. The switch may momentarily bolster public confidence, but ultimately such action is a cosmetic device which merely breeds greater distortions in the economy. Whether or not we have the will to solve the inflation problem is a question that lies much deeper than mere economics.

Our real task for the future is to rethink our basic goals. The most hopeful sign I have seen of late is that people in all walks of life—business, labor, and government itself—are beginning to rethink the functions of the government. We are beginning to ask ourselves in a serious way what governments should do and can do well, and what governments should not even try to do. But in a democratic society, of course, what government does is really only a reflection of what the people demand of it. As the Nobel laureate Friedrich von Hayek reminds us:

> Most people are still unwilling to face the most alarming lesson of modern history: that the greatest crimes of our time have been committed by governments that had the enthusiastic support of millions of people guided by moral principles. It is simply not true that Hitler or Mussolini, Lenin or Stalin, appealed to the lowest instincts of their people: they also appealed to some of the feelings which also dominate contemporary democracies.

Feelings aside, the reality is that the relationship of wages, prices, profits, losses, and deficits are all out of kilter—they no longer tell us the true value of anything. It is impossible to make rational business decisions when you do not know what anything is worth today, much less what it is likely to be worth tomorrow.

If we are to find lasting, long-term solutions to all these problems, we must start by telling ourselves the truth.

OBSERVATIONS FROM
THE GLOBAL ATTIC

· ■ ·

Gnomons, Words,
and Policies

. ■ .

So far as I know, history does not record the name of the person who first planted a stick in the ground and related the length of the shadow it cast with the time of day. The first crude gnomon was refined over the years and sundials were calibrated to show the hours. Eventually the measurement of time progressed from water clocks all the way to atomic clocks. Man's desire to measure time accurately has now reached the point where a ten-dollar quartz watch is more accurate than the most expensive timepiece that could be produced only a few years ago. Technology made the difference.

Skilled old craftsmen in the watch trade did not greet the advent of quartz technology with any great enthusiasm. The reigning experts knew that the way to build clocks was with levers and gears and not with silicon chips. This is not an unusual reaction to change, especially if it appears to threaten one's livelihood. While we still see sundials in the quiet gardens of the world, we order our lives with more exact timepieces.

The desire to measure things is a continuing phenomenon that runs the gamut from the quart of milk in the supermarket to detailed public opinion polls on every conceivable subject.

The best of the public opinion polls have been quite accurate in predicting elections, and while there have been misses here and there, on balance the record is fairly good. The best practitioners of this new art have learned to frame the question and interpret the answer to produce the best forecast.

The train of thought we all go through in the reasoning process is reflected in the words we use to describe the scene as we see it. While it's an ancient question whether or not we can think through a problem without using words, if we accept the thesis that words are at the very least helpful, then the meaning of those words becomes crucial in arriving at a good answer. Today I would argue that the words we use to describe and measure our economy no longer accurately reflect our society as it exists today.

Even very good people using bad information misjudge the situation. Since some very excellent economists have been dead wrong in their judgments about the future of the American economy, perhaps a case can be made that their mistakes may have flowed from using words and concepts that are no longer applicable to the real world. Most of the terms we use in standard economic analysis were invented in the industrial age, and while many are still relevant, some no longer measure what they once did, because the base has changed.

George Stigler, the Nobel laureate who has done such brilliant work on the consequences of economic policies, put it this way:

The first and the purest demand of society is for scientific knowledge, knowledge of the consequences of economic actions. . . . Whether one is a conservative or a radical, a protectionist or a free trader, a cosmopolitan or a nationalist, a churchman or a heathen, it is useful to know the causes and consequences of economic phenomena. . . . Such scientific information is value-free in the strictest sense; no matter what one seeks, he will achieve it more efficiently the better his knowledge of the relationship between action and consequences.

In order to get that information, we must have ways to measure things in some impartial manner. One of the principal sets of measures is published by our government. When George Jaszi retired recently, he left behind him the framework of the National Income and Products Accounts, which was first constructed in the midst of the Great Depression. The common wisdom about the American economy then was expressed by Franklin Roosevelt, who stated: "Our industrial plant is built. . . . Our task now is not discovery or exploitation of natural resources, or necessarily producing more goods . . . it is the soberer, less dramatic business of administering resources and plants already in hand." At that time our GNP was about $56 billion and our exports less than $500 million. The desire to regain the high employment levels of the late 1920s quite naturally affected the interpretation of the numbers. By any reckoning, the measurement of the GNP is an immensely difficult task, but today a case can be made that too much reliance on any single measure or concept of National Income Accounts puts one in real danger of missing one's economic forecasts. And what's far worse—bad economic policy.

It is no secret that in the last few years many very intelligent and skilled economists have badly missed predicting the direction of the U.S. economy. The puzzle is why. One reason may be that the measures we use in the National Income Accounts may no longer calibrate our society as accurately as they once did, because our world has changed so dramatically since they were formulated. This is a suggestion that may be greeted by economic practitioners with all the joy that watchmakers bestowed on the silicon chip.

Despite these hazards, it may be worthwhile to look more carefully at a few of the measuring sticks. First, the National Income Accounts don't have the same relevance they once had because they are strictly national in scope, although we now live in a global economy tied tightly together by telecommunications. Economic or political isolation is a thing of the past. The two wide oceans that were real barriers in George Washington's time can no longer perform this function. Data and voice transmissions now move with the speed of light via satellite and cable across the oceans, while ICBMs can bridge these bodies of water in minutes. The one world that Wendell Willkie wrote about in the 1940s, but never lived to see, is one of the central facts of our time.

What goes on in the world around us does not loom large in the numbers produced by National Income Accounts for the simple reason that they were not designed to capture it. At one time that was appropriate. Today, however, the global marketplace has moved from rhetoric to reality. Money and ideas can and do move to any place on this planet in seconds, and there is no longer any place to hide from the judgments of others. Bad economic policy in one nation is instantly known and reflected in the foreign exchange markets of the world. Major economic or political events anywhere in the world affect our economy directly or indirectly.

While this may seem self-evident, it is often not automatically a part of our reasoning process. In 1972, for example, when U.S. imports as a percent of GNP were only about half as large as today, many forecasters underestimated the sharp increase of inflation that followed in the wake of the dollar devaluation because they failed to appreciate the close interconnection. It makes as little sense today to look at the GNP of the United States without reference to the rest of the world, as it would to analyze the GNP of New York State without looking at the rest of the country. The Netherlands, with a population about the size of New York State, has its own GNP accounts, even though sensible policy analyses must proceed by looking at the rest of Europe as well. The deficits of European nations affect the American and other economies in a way not unlike our own deficit, since the money markets of the world are linked together electronically. In this connection, we should keep in mind that our deficit in the budgets of local, state, and federal governments combined is smaller, as a percentage of GNP, than those of all but one of our trading partners attending the economic summit.

The failure to understand the reality of the global market

helps explain why the crowding-out theory was never validated. People added up all the capital instruments sold on Wall Street in a year, and then took the amount of federal debt sold, and computed a ratio that purported to say that the federal government absorbed 20 percent, or whatever the number, of all capital raised. That ratio may once have been useful, but today it is a matter of complete indifference to the chief financial officer of any major company, whether one sells capital notes in New York, Hong Kong, or London. The market is not confined to Wall Street—it is the world. With the world's savings flowing across borders, National Accounts no longer give as accurate a view of the economy as they once may have. The failure to understand this massive change has caused more than a few economic forecasts to go awry.

Let me shift, for a time, from GNP to the notion of overall productive capacity, a concept that plays an important role in the formulation of monetary policy. Some economists reason that if industrial production is at, say, 85 percent of capacity, we are approaching the physical limits of output and thus we are in danger of starting up inflation. What these words do not tell you is that industrial production in the year 1985 employs only about 20 percent of American labor and that there is an almost infinite capacity to expand in the other nonindustrial sectors of our society. This was not always the case. The words we use are the words and reasoning we used when the majority of our labor force was employed in the industrial sector. These shifts of employment have been part of the American scene since our country started. Our farm population, for example, once constituted three-quarters of our working population. Even at the beginning of this century, more than one-third of us were farmers. When the last world war started, close to a quarter of our population lived on a farm. Today farmers constitute about 3 percent of our workers, but their productive capacity is the wonder of the world.

A not dissimilar phenomenon is taking place in manufacturing. The proportion of workers employed declined, but if we look at the volume of production, there has been almost no shift of consequence. In 1960, the output of goods accounted for about 45 percent of GNP, and it still remains in that range.

This relatively steady output, in the face of a massive exodus of workers from industry, raises the question of whether the figures on percentage of industrial capacity utilized mean the same thing for inflation as they once did. Indeed, this measure of capacity utilization played a key role in leading some forecasters to overestimate inflation in this current economic expansion. Another reason the capacity utilization index is misleading is that it covers only manufacturing, mining, and utilities, activities which account for a shrinking share of U.S. output. If it turns out that the ratio does not mean the same thing it used to, the question then becomes: Can we construct a new, more reliable measure for the kind of economy we now have?

Another word that is much in the news is productivity. How does America stack up in the global marketplace? Is the growth of American productivity greater or less than that of Japan or some other nation? These are important questions, but once again what do the words mean? When we talk about productivity, it used to mean, in its crudest terms, output per man-hour. While that is a useful concept in manufacturing, do we really have any meaningful measure of productivity in the information-intensive age, when the vast majority of our workers are employed in the service sector? The huge financial service industry is one example of the difficulty of measuring productivity. Once we get past counting the number of checks cleared per hour, or the number of insurance claims paid—all of which display greatly improved productivity, thanks to the computer—we then move immediately into the realm of the subjective. Is a loan officer's productivity in a bank or an insurance company or a credit company to be judged on the number of loans made, the size of the loans, the number of loans that are repaid on time, the quantity of bad debts created—or how do you measure productivity? No one really knows, even though many have tried. Although much work has been done in measuring productivity in steel and autos, industries that now employ less than 3 percent of our labor force, enough work may not have been done in other areas to give us great confidence in the production numbers.

Even in automobiles much has changed that the numbers do not capture. The cost of externalities has become a bigger factor. As Juanita Kreps has said:

> Henry Ford did not initially build a car equipped with seat belts or air bags, nor one designed to meet environmental standards. Now the need to protect safety and the environment makes it necessary for consumers to pay much higher prices—allegedly for cars but in fact the automobile buyer is paying in part for clean air. Without this externality, the price of the car would of course be much lower. But by including clean air in the price—which is probably the best way to exact payment—we obscure the enormous increase in productivity achieved in the output of automobiles.

If we think about our economy, another word we use is "capital." Economists of many schools tend to agree that capital is stored-up labor which has been expressed in dollars. A good case can now be made that knowledge and information are becoming the new capital in today's world. To suggest we examine this possibility does not mean the end of money capital, but it may throw a different light on the problem, so much discussed, of capital formation. To enter a business, the entrepreneur in the information age needs access to knowledge more than he or she needs large sums of money. To write the software program that may make the author millions of dollars may require only a relatively trivial sum of money, as compared to the amounts of money we used to think of as capital in entering, say, a heavy manufacturing business. On the other side of the coin, the knowledge capital accumulated in the software writer's head, or in the documentation, or on disks, is very substantial and very real. A strong argument can be made that information capital is as important, or even more critical, to the future growth of the American economy than money. Despite this perception, this intellectual capital does not show up in the numbers economists customarily look at or quote about capital formation.

If capital is what produces a stream of income—and that's a definition no one seems to quarrel with—then it follows that knowledge is a form of capital. And what's clear is that the formation of new knowledge is growing apace. Today it is accurate to say that at least 80 percent of all the scientists who ever lived are now alive, and that in our own country at least half of all scientific research done since the Revolution has been conducted in the last decade. With the total stock of knowledge doubling about every ten years, it is clear that our intellectual capital is being formed far more rapidly than tangible capital.

Even the numbers we use to describe tangible capital investment have some problems. Sometimes the figures may show that we are "disinvesting" when, in fact, what we are really doing is paying less money for much more capacity. We see this in our own lives in the ratio of price to capacity in the hand-held calculator, or the watch on your wrist, or the home computer on your desk. In saying that, I am not arguing that money capital will not continue to be very important; it will. But I am suggesting that the amazing accumulation of knowledge capital in the last twenty years is very substantial and growing every day, but it is uncounted. We have little or no control over the natural resources within our borders, but we do have control over our educational and cultural environment, which produces the men and women who have led, and will continue to lead, the world. If we want better economic forecasting and better policies, clearly some way needs to be found to crank the growth of knowledge into our equations.

In suggesting that it may be time to take a new look at many of the measures we use in assessing the economy, I am aware that almost every number we use has its constituency. Many labor contracts are tied to one inflation index or another, and shifting the content or the ratio of goods in the market basket would impact many people. The National Income Accounts, as presently constituted, are used by people in business, and any change in them might be upsetting, but nevertheless I believe that things really have changed.

A new world may require a new look at the way we calculate GNP, since today's method not only fails—except indirectly—to capture the benefits of rapidly accumulating knowledge; but is also marred by inconsistencies. For example, income is imputed to the owners of homes that they occupy, but there are no imputations for streams of services —real income, if you will—that emanate from autos, dishwashers, and other consumers' durables. In times of high taxation, durables—which are arguably capital investments—provide shelter, not only from taxes but often from the ravages of inflation. And there are other problems with GNP accounting, such as the overstatement of output that results from the treatment of capital consumption. If such conceptual omissions and errors affected only the accuracy of economic forecasts, there would not be so great a cause for concern. But that's not the case. GNP and productive capacity measures play a critical role in the formulation of the Federal Reserve's monetary policy.

What rightly concerns Fed policymakers is how fast the real economy can grow over the long haul without heating up inflation. Or to put it in the vernacular, what's the real potential growth rate for real GNP? The Fed, as nearly as I can infer from public statements, assumes GNP potential of around 3 percent, while some of their supply-side critics insist that it's as high as 5 percent. And since the difference between a 3 and a 5 percent potential could mean a huge difference in the level of real GNP over a ten-year span, the issue is anything but trivial.

Since the concept of potential GNP leans heavily on physical capital alone and productivity increases in the out years, it may be a dim star to steer by in today's world.

If knowledge capital is becoming relatively more important, we may be seeing a shift from an energy-intensive and materials-intensive economy to an information-intensive society. The current vocabulary of economics describes a world that still exists in part, but it may fail to capture the essential measures in this new world. My colleague John Reed invented the term in Citicorp of "investment spending," a concept it took us some time to understand, as it seemed at first glance to be a contradiction in terms. But it was and is appropriate to our times. Peter Drucker has said: "Indeed, in an information-based economy much of what we now consider 'expenditure' or 'social overhead' is actually 'capital investment,' and should—perhaps, must—produce a high return and be self-financing."

In suggesting we rethink and reexamine the shifting pattern of the elements which make up our economy, we are only taking a leaf out of the political book of the world.

We no longer look at maps published before 1931, when the Statute of Westminster was passed, giving formal recognition to the autonomy of the dominions of the British Empire. While the globe itself has not changed in an overall sense, the lines on the map of the world have been redrawn and dozens of new countries have been created. It would be folly to conduct our foreign policy based on the geopolitical map of 1930. It may be that conducting part of our economic policy based on measures that were valid in the 1930s carries similar hazards for us now.

Common Sense and
Technological Nonsense

■

Forty years ago, Wendell Willkie published a book entitled *One World,* which advanced the concept that the fate of each nation is inextricably intertwined with that of every other. That thesis, which seemed nothing more than a dream in the midst of the Second World War, is a truism now. The soaring vision of Jean Monnet in designing the Common Market, the birth of the United Nations, the World Bank, and the International Monetary Fund all moved us toward one world. But swift as were the politicians, technology moved still faster and further.

One result, little recognized by the general public, is that technology has combined with finance in a new and unique way that makes obsolete some of the old ideas of compartmentalized national markets, in much the same way that the advent of the tank in World War I and air power in World War II changed the concept of military power. In advancing this thesis, I am aware of the fact that General Billy Mitchell, who championed the theory of air power, was court-martialed for his trouble. It is also true that when the idea of using a tank in warfare was presented to Lord Kitchener, Britain's secretary of war during World War I, he dismissed it as "a pretty mechanical toy.'' The failure of the establishment—any establishment, be it the military, political, financial, or even scientific—to accept an idea that disturbs the old learning is a recurring theme in history. Ortega y Gasset reminds us that in June 1633, Galileo Galilei, then seventy years of age, was forced to kneel before the Inquisitional Tribunal of Rome and renounce the Copernican theory, a concept that was to make possible the modern science of physics. Politics were out of phase with science even in the seventeenth century.

Machiavelli, who knew something about such matters, put it this way:

> . . . it ought to be remembered that there is nothing
> more difficult to take in hand, more perilous to
> conduct, or more uncertain in its success, than to take
> the lead in the introduction of a new order of things.
> Because the innovator has for enemies all those who
> have done well under the old conditions, and lukewarm
> defenders in those who may do well under the new . . .

When the radio was invented and brought into commercial production, pundits opined that the phonograph was dead, that the record industry would be only a footnote in technological history. When television came along, we were told with equal certainty that the radio business was on the way out. None of this happened, because entrepreneurs in the electronics industry followed the targets of opportunity and created a world that was not as predicted.

Modern society is a mosaic made up of an ever-increasing number of these individual pieces, and the picture they create changes as fast as the pieces themselves. Charles Evans Hughes went to bed on election night in November 1916 secure in the knowledge that he had been elected President of the United States, only to be awakened to the unpleasant reality that California had voted for his opponent and the election had been lost. Now we watch newscasters on the major networks, with the help of computers, project the "winner" of our national election before people in the western states have had a chance to vote. Setting aside whether this development is good or bad for our democratic system, it is a clear example of how technology is affecting one of our basic institutions. Its political impact is enormous. So is its effect on many other aspects of our daily lives.

The new combination of science and finance produces some unease at present because often the consequences of scientific discoveries are not always anticipated. It is a well-established principle that a change of degree—if carried far enough—may eventually become a difference in kind. In biology, this is how new species are created and old ones die out. It can be argued that the speed of electronic information flow when it reaches sufficient velocity changes the nature of the transaction itself. Speed is what transforms a harmless lump of lead into a rifle bullet, or a collection of snapshots into a motion picture. When speed is combined with size in the financial markets, the numbers may rise to a point where they reach a critical size, and the market that's created becomes totally new and an integral part of our evolving world order. When this phenomenon is truly understood, the world can adjust, but first we must understand the magnitude and nature of change.

When I joined the international division of Citibank in the 1950s, instructions were clearly set forth that you never sent a cable if a letter would do, and the letter often went by sea mail. We took our first halting step toward the electronic age when we set up a telex line between the Citibank offices in New York and London. This circuit stuttered out about seven characters per second. Today, we have the capacity to transmit data at the rate of 152,300 characters per second. This is not just a change of form, it is a change of substance.

The flow of data around the world is now so huge and so diverse as to have worked a fundamental change in the world's economy. Every day, a computer system called CHIPS in the New York Clearing House processes the debits and credits of London Eurodollar trading in a volume approaching some two hundred billion dollars. Even by Washington standards, that is a very large number. This market is not just more of the same: it is something new in the world. It has changed the world.

People of all nations have long since adjusted to the grim reality that an intercontinental ballistic missile can travel from the Soviet Union to the United States, or a reverse path, in about thirty minutes, carrying enough explosives to render our society unlivable. We now have a less visible but perhaps equally profound challenge to the unlimited sovereign power of nation-states in the technical reality of global communications. Satellites have made communication costs almost insensitive to distance. There has been steady elimination of economic and technical barriers to the instantaneous exchange of information among peoples. This information is not always welcome and the political implications are enormous, even though barely visible on the horizon today. The luxury that some nations have permitted themselves of tight censorship has become increasingly difficult. The seventy commercial satellites currently circling the earth can now pump information from the skies to millions of transistor radios held in the hands of people who live in places that were once thought of as remote areas. It is not only news that is affected, because in the high-speed global transmission of digital data, the computer switching centers of the world make no distinction between the front page of the *Wall Street Journal,* the general ledgers of branches of multinational banks, or the television show you watch in your living room. They are riding, so to speak, in the same stagecoach. In fact, it is this technology that has made us a global community in the literal sense of that word. Whether we are ready or not, mankind now has a completely integrated international financial and informational marketplace capable of moving money and ideas to any place on this planet in minutes.

But the technological revolution poses thorny political problems. Since the digital information flowing in cables or moving through space will include such things as television shows, telephone conversations, and the stock market averages, all mixed together in a single stream, it becomes increasingly impossible to maintain any of the traditional distinctions between transmissions carrying news, entertainment, financial data, or even personal phone calls. This intermixing of data makes it even harder to pass laws restricting the transmission of one kind of information without impinging on the others. Streams of electrons are either free to move across national borders, or they are not.

What we are witnessing and participating in is a true revolution, and like all revolutions it is creating political unease. If a nation-state cannot control what its citizens see and hear, a little of the power of the state has slipped away even though a government might still force a modern Galileo to renounce scientific fact or decline a Nobel Prize.

Today, except in a very few instances, national borders are no longer defensible against the invasion of knowledge, ideas, or financial data. The Eurocurrency markets are a perfect example. No one designed them, no one authorized them, and no one controlled them. They were fathered by controls, raised by technology, and today they are refugees, if you will, from national attempts to allocate credit and capital, for reasons that have little or nothing to do with finance and economics.

America's ill-fated experiments with a so-called interest equalization tax provide another example. Designed to assist America's balance of payments, it gave instead great impetus to the Eurobond market and did little or nothing for the U.S. balance of payments. Eurobond issues placed in the public and private markets reached just under twenty billion dollars by the time the interest equalization tax was replaced, in July 1984. Once again, one nation's policies had unintentionally created a new international institutional market of such usefulness that it will not go away. The extent of capital flows depends only on the number of sophisticated investors.

What it all adds up to is a quantum jump in the efficient channeling of the world's capital flows. There are those who do not find this an altogether desirable development. The argument is heard that the very efficiency of the system undermines or complicates national monetary policy in particular countries.

Behind that argument lies a complaint by some governments that the existence of a free market disciplines them when they engage in overexpansionary policies, because the stream of electrons, increasing the mobility of money, makes it more difficult to ignore the one-world nature of financial life.

The old discipline of the gold standard has been replaced, in fact, by the discipline of the information standard. While the new control is not as harsh as the old automatic adjustment of gold shipment, it is in the end almost as certain. It is the successor to the Bretton Woods arrangement, with its pegged rates, where the marketplace punished overly inflationary countries through the loss of reserves. And even then, countries endeavored to maintain their freedom to inflate by imposing exchange controls. Efforts by some governments now to apply reserve requirements or other controls are only intended to mute the market's response to wide differences in domestic economic policies. Such moves carry with them grave risks for global financial stability. The very fact that the Eurocurrency market has been free has enabled it to act as a safety valve to the financial tensions and pressures inflicted by varying monetary and fiscal policies and such shock events as the OPEC oil price increases.

In his classic work on the gold exchange standard, Jacob Viner wrote that state intervention in private international markets leads "with a certain degree of inevitability to the injection of a political element into all international transactions." The presence of this political element, he noted, necessarily implies a "marked increase in the potentiality of economic disputes to generate international frictions." Politics and diplomacy will be substituted for more routine methods of settling commercial and economic disputes.

If governments and central banks now intervene more

actively to control international credit markets, it cannot be doubted that another fruitful source of political conflict among governments will thereby be opened up—along with the negative effects of such intervention on the economic efficiency of these markets.

A few years ago, I had an opportunity to demonstrate a small, portable plastic earth station. It was not hard to do. The disk was about the size of a large salad bowl and all I had to do was set it on the windowsill of a room on the top floor of Citibank headquarters in New York City. In less than a minute, a printer started to chatter out the Dow Jones running commodity report. As it happened, at that moment the Connecticut Bankers Association was suing to prevent us from opening an office for our finance company in one town in Connecticut. I could not help reflecting on the fact that we had just created what amounted to the basis for a commodity trading operation in less time than it took a Connecticut lawyer to get his legal pad out of the desk and start protecting his client's supposed monopoly.

In time, we got to open that one office in Connecticut, and that's still all we have there. Over the same time frame, we bought two transponders on the Westar Five satellite, now in orbit, and set up earth stations in more than a dozen cities throughout the U.S., which are handling the bank's domestic data flow. The course of these two events illustrates the mismatch between the rapid pace of technology and the determination of some to resist it.

The fact is that banking is a branch of the information business. One of the giants of the news industry, Baron Reuter, was among the first to grasp clearly the relationship between communications and finance. During the financial crisis and gold rush in Australia in early 1892, Reuter set up a money-by-cable remittance system that could transfer funds less expensively than did the commercial banks at that time. This service was profitable, and very popular with the public, but predictably unpopular with the banks.

Baron Reuter understood the fundamental relationships of

technology, money, and information, and so do his modern successors. A recent annual report of that international news agency reported that it was signing up thousands of subscribers a year for Reuter's monitor services throughout the world, and enabling dealers in the foreign exchange, money, securities, and commodity markets to retrieve the latest prices and news from Reuter's global computer system. Reuter is obviously still in the banking business and I, for one, have no objection. The baron would have been proud that his vision has been so clearly understood and implemented by his successors. Luckily, they are operating under the First Amendment and not the banking laws.

The irrationality of our regulatory approach to these matters can hardly be exaggerated. In a recent far-ranging review of new telecommunications and computer technology, *The Economist* put it this way:

> The distinction between telecommunications and computers is now technological nonsense. . . . Not bureaucrats, not lawyers, not customers, certainly not engineers—can say anymore where data-processing stops and message-carrying begins.

Our own Federal Communications Commission devoted seven years and millions of taxpayer dollars trying to maintain that distinction before finally giving up. That may prove to be the first time in history when a government agency had to refrain from regulating something because it couldn't define it.

No one has ever defined with any precision the business of banking, but the history of Reuter's gives us a clue. The history of innovative banking parallels that of the great news-gathering systems, for good banking like good journalism is based on sound information speedily delivered. In the sixteenth century, Jacob Fugger built the preeminent financial institution in Europe on fast couriers bringing news from agents stationed in Spanish America, Mediterranean Africa, and the Orient. The Rothschilds at the time of Napoleon built a legend and a fortune on the ability of their agents to obtain and transmit news by the fastest possible method.

Our current banking network, with its Euromarkets and its automated payments system, is not the cause of the world capital flows, but merely a means of transmission. It has become almost a book-entry system for part of the world. In fact, Henry Wallich, a governor of the Federal Reserve, has called it "the ultimate in intermediation between lenders and borrowers, between savers and investors."

This means of transmission of information and money is a primary cause of the fact that international banking is a system designed by fate to exist in a certain state of economic tension with all governments, including the most democratic. This tension is an ancient phenomenon dressed in electronic clothing.

Observing the achievements of the bankers of Amsterdam during the seventeenth century, a French philosopher, Charles de Montesquieu, congratulated them for having made it impossible for the princes of the world secretly to devalue their coinage. The standard of money can no longer be secret, he said, because the banker has learned to draw a comparison between all the money in the world, and to establish its just value.

Montesquieu did not think this activity would increase bankers' popularity with governments, and he warned of still another danger: By extending credit, banks had created a new species of wealth, and throughout history the princes of this world have rarely approved of wealth circulating outside their own control. There are countries, he observed, "where none but the prince ever had, or can have, a treasure; and wherever there is one, it no sooner becomes great than it becomes the treasure of the prince." There are few princes left in the world today, but only the vocabulary has changed. Governments now talk of "stateless money" instead of treasure, but the thought remains. There are still many countries where private banks are not welcome. Banks are unwelcome in Communist countries for precisely the reasons Montesquieu suggests: they furnish objective standards of measurement not easily subject to political pressures, and the banking system enables wealth to circulate in response to the true economic needs of the world, and not to political ukase or expediency. It is a system that no absolute monarch of Montesquieu's time, or totalitarian government of our own time, could or would live with. Because once a government accepts that system, it can no longer be absolute.

Today, this phenomenon can be observed as the Euromarket handles billions of dollars, deutsche marks, and other currencies subject to the jurisdiction neither of the country that issues the currency nor of the country where the transaction takes place. It does no good to wish that the technology had never been invented, and it won't go away. Just as the high seas are free to carry the world's commerce—stateless waters, if you will—so the Euromarkets are stateless markets to clear the world's financial transactions with a speed and an efficiency unmatched in history.

Modern technology has welded us into an integrated economic and financial marketplace which governments—and all of us—must learn to live with. The clock cannot be turned back, though the nature of this phenomenon is not as clear to the world's opinion-makers as it needs to be.

The beneficent results of low-cost, instantaneous international financial transactions, which we have almost begun to take for granted, are by no means appreciated in every quarter. Laws designed to control transborder data flows are being passed and many more are just over the horizon. All have laudable purposes—protecting privacy, for instance—but there are some people who suspect that, whatever the stated objective, proposed regulations of transborder electronic data flows are also coming more and more to look like old-fashioned economic nationalism.

As banks have grown into a global, interconnected financial network to meet the needs of a global marketplace, fears have been articulated that the system may be vulnerable—that it may be only as strong as its weakest link. This "weakest-link syndrome" proved unfounded when the Herstatt bank in Germany failed in 1974, but it exists—not only with regard to the payments systems but to make whatever point is the current topic of concern.

It is pointless to debate whether that perception is wholly true, partially true, or not at all true. Whether or not the system today is as fail-safe as it should be, it is not perceived as such by some people. The motives of these groups range from a philosophical distrust of what might be termed economic free speech in a truly efficient market, to genuine worries about the quality of credits being financed. Others, watching the worldwide inflation eat up the world's substance, look for something or somebody beyond their own national fiscal and monetary policy to blame. Whatever the motive, and regardless of whether the disquiet is real or imagined, until that perception is changed our doors will remain open to eager visitors who volunteer to help protect people's assets when what they really have in mind is controlling the flow of capital.

Since this tension between those who see the benefit of intermediation on an international scale and those who don't will continue, it behooves us in the private sector to make the system as efficient and safe as possible. We should make sure that the payments mechanism functions through good times and bad, that reciprocal currency lines are in place, and that there is a well-ordered cooperation with the world's central banks, which are themselves a major user of the market.

If those of us who are qualified to deal with improving the market do not respond, others will fill the vacuum. Much of what we must do is to make more explicit and more visible practices that already exist. As the perception grows that we live in a world of limited resources and unlimited demand, the world problem continues to be how to make maximum use of these resources. Helping to solve that problem has always been a banker's basic business—and with the tools now available, we have an opportunity for doing the job with a proficiency never seen before in history.

In fact, we are already doing it. What we have to defend is our right to continue to do so.

As world policy adjusts to these realities, so must we adjust and rethink how the world's financial system will function in the age of almost instant information. There is no longer anywhere in the world to hide. Even those countries that are self-sufficient in food, in energy, and in natural resources can no longer isolate themselves from the rest of the world. This state of affairs does not necessarily make the world an easier place in which to live. There are many days when buyers and sellers, politicians and bankers, all long for the past world of fixed exchange rates and for what seems in retrospect like simpler times. We are tempted to dream of the return to more compartmentalization of national security, when the castle wall constituted a real obstacle to the invader. But the progression of innovation is irreversible. Each new invention brings changed circumstances with which the world must cope. Edward III forever changed warfare at the battle of Crécy by introducing the Welsh longbow against the French. Today, the financial longbow is the linking of the satellite, the computer, and the cathode ray tube. The kind of world that existed in July 1944, when the United Nations Monetary and Financial Conference gathered at Bretton Woods, New Hampshire, has changed so much as to be almost unrecognizable. The nature and distribution of economic and military power has changed dramatically, and this, combined with the new technology, has destroyed many of the old arrangements. We all have our own investments of intellectual capital in things as they were yesterday, and sometimes even a compulsion to preserve them in the face of all evidence to the contrary. To recognize in a clear-eyed way the existence of an international information standard is not in any sense to denigrate the achievements of the old fixed exchange rates of Bretton Woods any more than taking the Concorde to New York denigrates the achievements of the clipper ships. It is simply a different world. There is a time and a place for everything. As Thomas Hobbes once said: "Hell is truth seen too late."

The truth is that there is a new phenomenon in the world and one with which we have to deal. There exists a global marketplace for ideas, money, goods, and service that knows no national boundaries. The beggar-thy-neighbor policies originally developed by Colbert and still pursued by some governments, often urged on by their merchants and industrialists, can no longer work. We now have a new calculus which, I believe, will in the end be beneficial to the world. It exerts global pressure on all governments to pursue sounder economic policies because it is becoming increasingly obvious that it is now impossible to hide in our new electronic world.

There are some who find this disconcerting, and no doubt it has unwanted side effects. Markets can and do overreact until fact can be sorted out from fiction, often at great cost. Maybe life was easier in the age of the homing pigeons, but the hard truth is that the genie will not go back into the bottle and the scientific advances are irreversible. Modern gold—or the liquid capital of our citizens—will flow in or out of our countries in response to information, as did gold itself in other times. It is up to us all to learn how better to manage our affairs so that we may benefit from the new technology, and not be hurt by it.

The Great Whale Oil Syndrome

▪ ■ ▪

Few Americans even remember that from the time of the American Revolution until the Civil War, a major source of artificial lighting was the whale oil lamp. No one needed a congressional commission to predict that the supply of whale oil could not forever keep pace with the demand of a growing nation.

The tragedy of our Civil War disrupted whale oil production, and its price shot up to $2.55 a gallon, almost double what it had been in 1859. Naturally, there were cries of profiteering and demands for Congress to "do something about it." The government, however, made no move to ration whale oil or to freeze its price, or to put a new tax on the "excess profits" of the whalers who were benefiting from the increase in prices. Instead, prices were permitted to rise. The result, then as now, was predictable. Consumers began to use less whale oil and the whalers invested more money in new ways to increase their productivity. Meanwhile, men with vision and capital began to develop kerosene, other petroleum substitutes, and innovations based on technology. The first practical generator for outdoor electric lighting was built in 1875, the forerunner of an entire new industry that would change forever the way we would light our homes. By 1896, the price of whale oil had dropped to forty cents a gallon. Whale oil lamps were no longer in vogue; they sit now in museums to remind us of the impermanence of crisis. This cycle, repeated in thousands of instances, demonstrates the truism that the progress of the world never runs in a straight line. In reality, all of life is a series of crises, some of which can be foreseen but many of which cannot. Pundits would prefer that the world were more predictable, but their straight-line projections are almost always upset by the untidy balancing of competing forces at work. These adjustment processes work to achieve rough equilibrium because most sectors of society have a vested interest of one kind or another in making them function. Since this long, mostly uneventful, adjustment process does not lend itself to ominous stories, and lacks a dramatic denouement on which to hang a headline, it passes with little attention.

Examples abound, but the great OPEC oil crisis is a classic case in point. When OPEC first embargoed some oil shipments and dramatically lifted crude oil prices in 1974, the air was heavy with forebodings of doom. The schism between economic interdependence and political independence was thrown into stark relief. There was a horror movie for every taste, ranging from the specter of a worldwide blackout to the more modest suggestion that massive defaults would occur in loans to less developed countries. Front-page stories in respected newspapers suggested that massive defaults would in turn pull down international financial institutions. The world, we were told, was in for a rerun of the Great Depression of the 1930s. This doomsday story was told with great skill, and told over and over again. It sold a lot of newspapers and not a few books, but it overlooked the fact that individuals and nations can, and do, act and react to protect what they perceive to be their own self-interest. This is what makes the adjustment process work.

Actually, the energy crisis was made in Washington. A scarcity of energy in the United States was assured as early as

1954, when Congress empowered the Federal Power Commission to set an artificially low wellhead price on natural gas to be used in interstate commerce. This low price ceiling overstimulated consumer demand for natural gas and discouraged exploration for new oil supplies in the United States —an infallible guarantee of an eventual shortage. It was akin to the plowing under of surplus crops of the 1930s, only on a grander scale.

When the first OPEC oil crisis occurred in 1973, there was immense anxiety over both a shortage of domestic oil and a surplus of money flowing to the Middle East oil-producing states. What happened, of course, is that the OPEC countries deposited their cash surpluses in American and European banks, which re-lent them to borrowers in other countries, especially developing countries that had no other means of meeting their increased oil bills. Along with these funds, members of the international banking community became the recipients of much gratuitous advice, usually from the same people who were devising new ways to regulate the oil markets, urging us in the financial markets to follow their example. Had we done so, the world's financial markets would have become as chaotic as the world's oil markets, and it is entirely possible that everyone's worst fears might have been realized. Instead, we adhered to what we knew were traditional principles of sound banking, and the successful adjustments to the quadrupling of oil prices in 1973 and 1974 became one of the most dramatic episodes in economic history. There was no historical precedent for such a massive transfer of financial assets, and the majority of commentators, including most of the "experts," were pessimistic about the future of the world international monetary system.

The world, however, refused to follow the doomsday scenario. The annual OPEC surplus—which increased tenfold in a single year—began declining in 1975 and disappeared by 1978. After the initial jolt, the developing countries' economies were soon growing nearly as fast as before. The widely prophesied catastrophe failed to materialize, because the prophets of calamity ignored several inconvenient facts. One such fact is that there are fifteen non-OPEC developing countries that account for three-fourths of all debt owed to banks in industrial countries. Before the first oil shock, the average deficit on their current accounts—the excess of what they were paying for their imports over what they were getting for their exports—was running about 2 percent of their gross national products. That might be considered the normal situation of the more successful less-developed countries before the price of oil went up.

There is nothing wrong, or even unusual, about that ratio. Countries import capital in order to speed their economic development. The capital inflow permits a higher level of domestic investment and more economic growth than would have occurred without it. It adds to the countries' capacity to repay at the same time that it increases their external debt. This is the regular situation of a successful private firm—and of a successful developing country. It is an accurate description of the United States of America from colonial days up to about 1915. It is a hallmark of progress.

The caveat is that the imported capital must be used to create new domestic economic activity sufficient to at least cover the carrying charge on the debt. What worried many analysts after the first oil shock was that even the most successful countries would now use so much of their borrowed money to pay for oil that they would not generate the economic growth needed to service the debt.

There was a period of two years—1974 and 1975—when these fears might have appeared justified. The current account deficit of the major LDCs increased nearly eighteen billion dollars. The oil price rise accounted for about a third of that deterioration; the other two-thirds was due mainly to the prolonged recession in the United States, Europe, and Japan, which cut prices and held down the volume of LDC exports.

But at the same time, the OPEC countries began spending their surpluses rapidly. During 1974–1978, imports of goods and services by the OPEC countries were roughly equal to three-fourths of their exports. Almost everyone underestimated how fast governments could spend money—even though we should all know better. The OPEC surplus was further curbed by the slowing in the growth of oil consumption in the oil-importing nations. The real price of oil increased only about 4 percent from mid-1974 to early 1977 and then actually declined 4.5 percent by the end of 1978.

All this was exactly what an old-fashioned economist might have predicted. But somehow it came as a great surprise to a remarkable number of other people—especially to the people whose business in life is to regulate, and who still do not understand that the world has become one huge financial marketplace.

At the time of the first OPEC price increases, there was already in place a Eurocurrency market and a Eurobond market capable of absorbing both the short-term and the long-term investments of the newly rich oil producers many times over.

As a result, the sixty-billion-dollar increase in the OPEC surpluses found itself quickly absorbed into a market estimated in gross terms at more than three hundred billion dollars at that time, where it caused hardly a ripple—to the astonishment of those who had not anticipated the growth of Euromarkets any more than they had anticipated the oil price increases.

Because projections of disaster were so pervasive at the time of the oil shock, even some of the greatest professionals in the business have expressed mild surprise at the speed and relative smoothness of the adjustment process. The former managing director of the International Monetary Fund, Johannes Witteveen, remarked that the problem of the oil crisis was overcome "rather better than we thought possible at the time."

One reason is that world trade continued to grow faster than world commodity output. The value of world exports by 1981 was almost two trillion dollars. The continued growth of world trade and international capital markets produced a rapidly expanding foreign exchange market, now estimated at fifty trillion dollars a year.

While markets were straining to handle the unprecedented transfers of financial reserves, and doing it successfully, each nation reacted to the oil crisis in its own way. No one decision or policy was right for every nation stunned by the oil shock. Some oil-importing countries retrenched their economic development plans, to ride out the storm. Others, like Brazil, turned to global capital markets for financial support while permitting their internal policy adjustments to take effect. Not every nation had in place the requisite economic policy that could attract and hold private capital to bridge the gap. But those that took on the added burden of the oil crisis, yet pressed ahead with sound internal economic development plans, have not regretted it. While each nation reacted in its own way, each learned from others. This is so because every nation on this earth that is successful in advancing the welfare of its people borrows heavily on the experience, technology, and capital of others. What cannot be borrowed, of course, is the determination, the self-confidence, and the courage to manage a crisis.

One of the most reassuring omens for the future is the abundant self-confidence and determination demonstrated by the oil-dependent economies of the less developed countries in meeting that challenge of higher energy costs.

Despite predictions to the contrary, all the wealth of the world did not wind up in OPEC hands. The international reserves of the non-oil-producing LDCs did not decline but rather increased and the current account surplus of OPEC fell sharply in the aftermath of the first oil shock. The second OPEC price increase, in 1979, was followed by a similar reduction in the OPEC surplus, and by 1982 the current account surplus was near zero. This reality was very different from the strident forecasts of doom; in fact, just the opposite happened. The non-oil developing countries increased their export earnings from $82 billion in 1973 to $327 billion in 1981. In the course of this extraordinary explosion of exports, coupled with increased borrowing on international credit markets, they added some $60 billion to their total international reserves. Once again the conventional fears of the prognosticators turned out to be wrong.

Instead, a rather different problem developed. The counterpart of oil import dependency is, of course, oil export dependency. As we struggled with our problems of import dependency, oil-exporting countries perceived a need to reduce their excessive dependence on oil exports. In 1977, oil accounted for about 97 percent of all merchandise export revenues for the Gulf states and approximately 87 percent for the other OPEC countries. Awareness of this heavy reliance led various OPEC countries to undertake costly industrial development programs while they still had enough oil in the ground and assured markets around the world.

As OPEC's annual spending on imported products, consultants, freight, contractors, and other services began to exceed its rate of increase in oil revenues, its so-called oil surplus shrank accordingly. What could not be usefully spent on imported goods and services was made available for international investment. By year-end 1981, about $450 billion had been reinvested directly or indirectly in the economies of other countries.

Large international commercial banks contributed to fostering this trend by extending credit across national borders to private, quasi-private, and governmental borrowers. This credit took the form of short-, medium-, and long-term financing in the form of loans, letters of credit, guaranties, and securities underwriting and distribution, all subject, whatever the form, to the adjustment mechanisms should trouble arise.

The expansion in international commerical bank loans (excluding interbank loans) was about 20 percent a year, adjusted for inflation, between 1964 and 1978. In the same period, world trade grew 7.5 percent a year and world production 5.25 percent a year, also adjusted for inflation. Since 1978, all of these magnitudes have grown more slowly, but international commercial bank loans have continued to grow a great deal faster than world trade, while world trade has continued to grow faster than world production. Thus world trade is becoming a larger share of output and international commercial bank lending is growing faster than both. Commercial bank lending now accounts for a much larger part of total international capital flows than any other private source of funds.

Since international lending is such an important part of the global economy, it might be interesting to examine some of the technical aspects of how credit and the adjustment mechanisms operate.

Usually a transaction starts with an institutional borrower in one country approaching one or more private commercial banks in another country for a loan. It may well happen that banks will organize several syndicates and offer prospective borrowers competing financing proposals. The borrower may be a private corporation, an agency of a government, or a government itself. The terms of the loan proposal are reviewed, negotiated, agreed upon, and put in writing. The documentation will state the purpose, currency, and principal amount of the loan; the interest payable; the repayment terms; the nature and extent of any guaranties or collateral; and the respective additional promises or restrictions to be observed by the borrower.

The loan agreement, depending on the laws involved and the complexity of the transaction, can run from one page to hundreds of pages. Whatever the length, the loan agreement almost invariably provides that if the borrower—whether private corporation, governmental agency, or government—fails to comply with one or more of its obligations, then a "default" occurs. That default has no significance in itself—it has either occurred or it has not occurred.

A default can come about in several ways—a failure to pay principal or interest when due, a failure to observe a covenant, or a failure in payment of indebtedness owed to other lenders. In any such event, the lending bank or banks have several options: (1) to do nothing, but without prejudicing rights to take later action; (2) to expressly waive the default and, perhaps, revise the loan agreement by rescheduling the dates and/or amounts of principal and/or interest payments or redrafting one or more of the applicable covenants; or (3) to declare the entire debt to be immediately due. This last alternative is commonly called an "acceleration" of the debt.

Whichever course the lenders follow, the debt remains outstanding. If the lending bank or banks elect to accelerate the debt and the debtor does not pay in full, they have available a number of remedies. If they hold deposits of the debtor, they can "set off" these deposits up to the amount of the debt —that is, subtract the amount owed from the borrower's bank balances on deposit. This was the case in the Iranian debt acceleration. If the banks hold guaranties or collateral for the debt, they can proceed against the guarantors or foreclose on the collateral. If they have neither deposits, guaranties, nor collateral, the banks can try to locate property belonging to the debtor and attempt to seize and sell it by appropriate legal process. The acceleration of debt by one lender, or group of lenders, will almost certainly lead to the acceleration by other lenders as they take similar steps to protect their position as creditors.

Whether the debtor is a private corporation, government agency, or government, the lending banks can use all available legal remedies both in and out of the debtor's domicile. However, since legal proceedings brought in local courts of the borrower's country may, for reasons of national interest, be ineffective (or at best slow), the banks usually include in the loan agreement provisions by which the borrower agrees to submit to legal action in courts outside the debtor's home country. These provisions often include waivers of the defense of sovereign immunity, consents to attachment, and agreements that a "neutral" body of law will apply to these external legal actions. Increasingly, as disciplines in the international lending arena tighten, banks are insisting on provisions of this type and government agencies and governments that seek access to private financial markets are willing to accept them.

Private corporate borrowers and some incorporated government-agency borrowers that find themselves unable to pay their debts or to persuade their lenders to reschedule, on their own initiative or that of the lenders, may become subject to bankruptcy proceedings. These proceedings, usually conducted in the courts of the borrower's home country—and possibly subject to motives of national self-interest—may result in either a mandatory rescheduling of the debt or a liquidation of the borrower and a distribution of its assets to its creditors.

However, there is simply no mechanism for a national government to be thrown into bankruptcy proceedings. This is inherent in the nature of national governments, which are not liquidated even under the most adverse financial situations. They often find themselves in extremely weak financial situations, with all kinds of domestic and international repercussions. However, they do not cease to exist. They are not liquidated. Sooner or later they get their act together, often because better financial managers are brought into the government. At such times, the International Monetary Fund is very useful in suggesting creative fiscal and monetary policies for the government borrower and suggesting a debt rescheduling as part of these policies. The whole process is, however, voluntary.

On occasion, into this rather orderly world of the legalities of international bank lending there may enter unanticipated events which dramatically change the nature of the relationships between the lender banks and the borrowers. For example, governments, usually as a result of a revolution or other internal disturbance, enact domestic laws disavowing or making it illegal to pay external debts of the former government. Russia did this in 1917, Germany in 1934, and Cuba in 1960. Or governments having jurisdiction over some lender banks may use the credit and deposit relationship with a foreign government and its corporations to exert economic pressure. England did this with Rhodesia in 1962, and the United States with Iran in 1979. When such events occur, the private lender banks have no alternative but to adjust to these government interventions as best they can. For instance, unless specifically prohibited by applicable law, the banks can seek to exercise their available remedies of setting off, exercising rights against guarantors or collateral, and attaching debtors' external assets where they can be found.

But usually after a period of time, which may be as short as a few years as in the case of Iran, or as long as several decades as in the case of Germany and Russia, intergovernmental or private agreements are reached under which debt service is resumed on an adjusted basis or the debt is settled at a reduced amount. The result of a governmental borrower's refusal to pay or settle its debts is exclusion from the international credit system, an option borrowers can ill afford over the long haul. An illustration of a typical trade transaction in today's interdependent world shows why this is so. Natural gas owned by Indonesia's oil agency, Pertamina, flows out of a well discovered by Royal Dutch Shell into a liquefaction plant designed by French engineers and built by a Korean construction company. The liquefied gas is loaded onto U.S.-flag tankers, built in U.S. yards after a Norwegian design. The ships shuttle to Japan and deliver the liquid gas to a Japanese public utility, which uses it to produce electricity that powers an electronics factory making television sets that are shipped aboard a Hong Kong–owned containership to California for sale to American farmers in Louisiana who grow rice that is sold to Indonesia and shipped there aboard Greek-flag bulk carriers. All of the various facilities, ships, products, and services involved in the complex series of events are financed by U.S., European, and Japanese commercial banks, working in some cases with international and local governmental agencies. These facilities, ships, products, and services are insured and reinsured by U.S., European and Japanese insurance companies. Investors in these facilities, ships, products, and services are located throughout the world. This illustration is not only factual, it is typical of transactions that take place over and over again daily throughout the globe. Only members of the international financial system can play.

Finally, it is worthwhile to understand how commercial banks and their regulators deal with the financial reporting of international loans, both those in good standing and those not so.

International commercial loans, as well as all other loans, are carried on the asset side of a bank's balance sheet at 100 percent of principal amount, and the interest on them is accrued periodically on the bank's income statement, irrespective of the dates of actual interest payment so long as the loans are not in default on payment of principal or interest.

If an international commercial (or, for that matter, any other) borrower fails to make an interest payment on schedule, the loan is put on a so-called nonaccrual or nonperforming basis for *income* reporting purposes. Unless there is specific reason to believe that the principal of the loan will not ultimately be paid in full, the loan (even if on a nonaccrual basis) will continue to be carried at 100 percent of principal amount as an *asset* on the balance sheet.

When a loan, international or otherwise, fails to meet both interest and principal payments, the lender bank, and its regulators and auditors, face a judgment call as to whether the loan should properly be regarded as an asset at full principal amount. If they feel the loan is unlikely to be paid in full, they will "reserve against" it on the balance sheet. This is done by charging (reducing) the bank's bad-debt reserve by an amount equal to the doubtful portion of the loan and at the same time reducing the assets on the bank's balance-sheet doubtful portion on the loan—or "writing off" the doubtful amount. As rapidly as possible, the bad-debt reserve is replenished by making charges against the bank's profits. This would affect the bank's stockholders, but not impact the financial system since the bad-debt reserves are ample for almost any contingency.

If repayment of the entire amount of the loan is in doubt, the process is the same, except that the loan is totally removed from the asset side by an equal offsetting charge to the bad-debt reserve. This removal of a loan from the asset side of the balance sheet is frequently referred to as "writing off" the loan.

However, the legal treatment of a loan that has been "reserved against" or "written off" is fundamentally different from its accounting treatment.

For accounting purposes, the loan's "nonaccrual," "reserved against," or "written off" status is reported to regulators, depositors, and investors of the bank at a conservative but fair evaluation of the troubled loan.

For legal purposes, however, the loan continues to exist as a debt of the borrower—without regard to how the bank chooses to treat it in its accounting. The bank is free to continue efforts to reschedule or collect the loan in any way it can for as long as it wishes. Historically, at least 40 percent of such loans is ultimately collected. Only when the bank judges the expenses involved in collecting a loan to exceed the potential recovery is a loan completely abandoned. Even then, if the abandoned loan is to a government, the *memory* of the defaulting borrower's behavior and costs to the bank remain.

Not surprisingly, it is this last intangible factor—the memory of past poor credit behavior—that is probably the best deterrent against the temptation of governments, which cannot go bankrupt, to default or repudiate their debts. Access to international credit markets is essential to countries so that their citizens can obtain the wealth of goods, materials, services, and technology that is available in the world. It is impossible, as a result of the telecommunications revolution, to keep people from knowing what is produced and available in other parts of the world. If governments, through their own mismanagement, ruin their international creditworthiness and thus their access to world markets, it is not unlikely that their citizens will someday choose to select governments with better management capability.

These realities are well known to international borrowers —be they governments, government agencies, or private corporations—and the threat of exclusion tempers in time even the rashest passions of the moment. Consequently, borrowers have always chosen to use the adjustment mechanisms built into the system when debt problems arise, as they invariably will from time to time.

The central lesson to be learned by looking back at the early days of the oil crisis from the perspective of a dozen years —and at the other problems that have arisen since then—is that it proves once again that tomorrow will not simply be today twenty-four hours older. Tomorrow will be the product of a vast number of pragmatic decisions, random events, and minor moves, all of which, when taken together, build or destroy our global economy.

The lesson is almost as old as history: Any country that continues to make the difficult decisions needed to control inflation, and that opens its economy to global markets and lets the market price mechanism function, will continue to find willing partners among the world's major commercial banks, and the banks will find them worthy credit risks.

To say that there are reasonable grounds for expecting the debt burden of the developing countries to remain manageable is not to say that we have nothing to think about. Private lenders are unlikely to forget the Middle East war and the Iranian revolution and the political turmoil in Central America. They may be expected to build those memories into their credit policies and the interest rates they charge. That is known as evaluating risk, and it is what bankers get paid for. Events of the past dozen years would seem to suggest that we have been doing our job reasonably well. Remember, it was not the highly publicized LDCs that caused the huge loan write-offs at the banks in the 1970s; it was the made-in-America real estate investment trusts. While the pundits were predicting horrendous defaults in loans to LDCs, the American banking system instead was writing off billions of dollars of bad loans on good old American real estate. Somehow, that never made as good copy as the losses that did not occur. From the first round of OPEC price increases until today, U.S. banks have had a lower average loss experience on foreign credits than on their domestic loans.

Discussing these matters early in 1980, the chairman of the board of governors of the Federal Reserve System, Paul Volcker, concluded his remarks with an observation with which I agree:

> I cannot leave this subject without commenting on the enormous problems of economic management in the United States, and in every oil-consuming country. . . . Even without the difficulties caused by recent pricing and production decisions, we would have needed to accommodate a vast change in the way we use and produce energy. . . . The recycling process has worked smoothly to date—the real process of adjustment less so. Let us not delude ourselves: financial flows cannot fill indefinitely a gap that must be covered by conservation, production, and new forms of energy. Our past success in recycling—and the role it can play today—must not lead us to stretch that process to the breaking point.

What Mr. Volcker was saying, if I understand him correctly, is that you cannot expect your banker to solve all your problems. Nor, I might add, can they be solved by getting angry at Arabs or at Texas oil companies. They will only be solved when the industrialized world finally faces up to the fact that the golden age of cheap oil is gone forever.

What really happened in 1973 and 1974 is that we finally got a long-overdue bill. We paid it, and now we are engaged in a process of learning to live within our means. It is not the end of the world. In fact, the old copybook maxim used to tell us that this was the first prerequisite for getting rich. It still works.

As it turned out, what we saw was that the world money markets now have the necessary flexibility and strength to sustain almost any economic adjustment process. Furthermore, the world's total financial structure is now a unified system, and while the international flow of funds may be impeded from time to time by political tensions, no one nation or group of nations can successfully pursue unilateral policies without regard for the whole international community.

There could scarcely be a sharper contrast with what happened then, and since, in the world's oil markets. In the United States, the crude oil entitlements program enacted in 1973, for instance, was supposed to distribute the benefits of low-cost domestic oil to all refiners. One of the first results was to subsidize the importation of foreign oil and remove most of the incentive for oil refiners to search for new domestic sources, because they believed that, in the end, the government would effectively make crude oil available to all refiners at roughly the same price.

Every year some 2,500 ships discharge crude oil into more than 600 U.S. refineries and import terminals. Just moving the crude around to get the right grades to the right locations requires dozens of trades. If the government continues down the path of substituting central planning in Washington for the interplay of forces in the market, the lines in front of the gas stations we witnessed in 1973 and again in 1979 may be remembered as part of the good old days. The gas lines, you may recall, were largely the result of the Department of Energy's action in mandating the refining of too much heating oil instead of gasoline, then allocating the available gasoline to politically influential groups such as farmers, and finally allocating what was left in such a way that ski resorts were awash with gasoline in June while nobody along the coasts could drive to the beach.

This is the same wisdom that many would like to see brought to the world's financial markets. So far, however, the world capital markets have managed systematically to readjust themselves and preserve the world's economic balance without waiting for governments to tell them how to do it. This is extremely fortunate, because what can be done by a free market is almost always far more than the planners and regulators believe possible.

The oil crisis was not the first, nor will it be the last, dislocation in our global economy that produces headlines. Indeed, in quick order during the following years, flurries of concern surfaced over the external debt of Zaire, Nicaragua, Costa Rica, and Turkey, rising to higher levels of anxiety over Iran, then Poland, and most recently Argentina, Brazil, and other South American countries.

All of these events immediately triggered a series of actions which put the infinitely complex adjustment process in motion. Equilibrium is restored in the system in ways that planners can never foresee. It is difficult to conceive of a computer program which could even record, let alone factor in, the infinite variety of actions and reactions which will be taken by individuals and nations in their own self-interest. But, during the early days of those crises, anyone who did not join in the cry to "do something" was perceived as either a person who did not understand the problem or a Pollyanna. Being a Pollyanna and a successful banker are mutually exclusive. Sound banking is based on assembling as many reliable facts as possible. Instead of joining the chorus of despair, we examine and reexamine our international lending criteria. We watch and study how the markets are adjusting. Other responsible international bankers do the same. We stay in the business and together with the international monetary agencies supply funds to buy time for the adjustment process to work.

We have long since passed the fork in the road of history where the world can return to economic nationalism and isolationism. We know with great clarity that a major event anywhere in the world will impact us all. Our fates are inextricably intertwined and the beggar-thy-neighbor policy of times past has lost whatever doubtful utility it may once have had.

The reality of economic interdependence in no way lessens the importance of independent initiative by men and by nations. Each nation has to evolve its own system that is right for it in bettering the human condition of its own people. We have on this planet every kind of political system, from a tribal council in some of the newer countries to centralized all-pervasive government planning in others. In between these two extremes one can find functioning governments reflecting every shade of the political spectrum. The only constant factor is change as each society moves at its own pace along the curve of its own history. We have moved a very long way in our country from the collectivism expressed in the Mayflower Compact, which governed absolutely the lives of our first settlers, to our current complex pluralistic democracy.

In between the Mayflower Compact of 1620 and today, we have experienced in the United States everything from a destructive civil war, which brought with it martial law, to decades during which whole areas of our western frontier had no law at all. The oceans, which helped to protect our isolation, have long ceased to be barriers. In short, the luxury of economic independence is substantially gone from the world, and all kinds of political and economic systems are caught in the same web of interdependence.

What, then, is the lesson of the last dozen years? Certainly we cannot assume that tomorrow will be any more safe and uneventful than yesterday. On the contrary, all history validates the prophecy in the Scriptures that "in the world ye shall have tribulations." The shape of coming events is unknown, and we have all learned that the balance of the world's economy can be suddenly and severely disrupted. We have also come to realize that even under crisis conditions the global adjustment process works. It is what saved us in the past and gives us confidence in the future.

We Were an LDC Once Too

■ ■

The worry beads labeled "loans to less developed countries" have been rubbed bare, and needlessly so. Some of the rhetoric of concern flows from various forums of Third World gatherings, some from scholarly studies, and a lot from the pages of our daily newspapers. It is produced by people with short memories or near vision who see only problems. In the course of my banking career, I've lent money to France, Britain, Italy, and about every country in Latin America, and at the time each borrowed it was in bad shape, otherwise none would have had to borrow. All those loans were repaid in time. That experience is not unique.

The drumfire of criticism of loans and investments to developing countries is a far cry from the genuine excitement that greeted President Kennedy's announcement of the Alliance for Progress. It was only yesterday when our government was urging the private sector to assist the developing world. Our present climate of accusatory rhetoric is apparently designed to prove that we did in fact heed President Kennedy's words.

In the atmosphere thus created, the general public, which often gets its expert advice through the newspapers, has understandably formed some erroneous and potentially dangerous opinions about helping the developing countries. It is widely believed, for example, that all LDCs are poor; that money and capital are the same thing; and that banks can make loans whenever and wherever they choose. Perhaps the greatest contribution one can hope to make in this situation is to return to fundamentals and attempt to define what it is we are talking about.

Calling a dog a horse does not change it into a horse even if done in a firm voice or on nationwide television. But labels are important. The mathematician Pascal once wrote that "definitions are never subject to contradiction . . . nothing is more permissible than to give whatever name we please to a thing." In view of this, he said, "we must be careful not to take advantage of our freedom to impose names by giving the same name to two different things."

Part of our problem now is that we have indeed given the same label not only to two but to many diverse nations. The term "less developed countries" lumps together India with its six hundred million people and Singapore with fewer than three million; Tanzania, where nine out of ten people live in the country, and Argentina, where eight out of ten live in the cities; Brazil with annual gross national savings of more than fifteen billion dollars and Sri Lanka with less than four hundred million dollars in gross national savings.

Another commonly ignored fact about developing countries is that each nation in this diverse group is at a different stage of development, and has vastly different resources and national goals. Per capita income, in the non-oil-producing LDCs, ranges from a low of ninety dollars in Bangladesh to a high of ten thousand six hundred dollars in New Caledonia.

What many LDCs do have in common is a desire to accelerate their growth in order to raise the living standards of their citizens, while at the same time they share an inability to generate enough internal savings to finance that acceleration. Their chronic need for foreign investment and credit is something for which they deserve more praise than criticism. It is testimony to their concern for the welfare of their own people. Stagnant, poor societies that do not worry about raising their people's living standards do not perceive that they have capital shortages. Historically, in fact, the stagnant countries have been the best places to hoard gold, collect diamonds, and build palaces.

The developing countries, which do want to raise the lot of their citizens, have been assisted in their efforts by large transfers of resources from the industrialized countries ever since the Second World War. The nature of those transfers has evolved steadily over that period of time. In the beginning, most aid took the form of grants to former colonies. This was followed by official loans on concessionary or preferential terms. In almost every instance, however, as soon as a country created conditions which made it possible to borrow commercially, it began turning to commercial banks and other private financial institutions. By the end of 1967, the share of lending by private creditors in the total external public debt of the LDCs had risen to about 30 percent, and it is now probably in the neighborhood of 40 to 45 percent.

Whether this trend toward private financing will continue cannot be predicted with certainty, since no one can be sure what policies governments might choose to adopt. But to the extent that normal economic forces are permitted to operate, private international finance will undoubtedly continue being increasingly important to the LDCs. Since there will be a strong continuing need for the developing countries to attract more external capital than official sources can hope to provide, private capital will move toward those countries that manage their affairs in such a way as to be a good credit risk.

Bear in mind that in the United Nations classifications there are only seven industrial countries in the world, about fourteen more are called semi-industrial, and all the rest are developing.

There are five different kinds of loans that banks make to these countries, almost all very short term, and it is important to differentiate among them. Newspapers say Citibank, or

Chase, or Morgan, or whoever, has fifty million dollars in loans to Italy. That's like saying Bank of America has fifty million dollars in loans in New York City. It means absolutely nothing. When the figures are taken apart, you find that the bank has fifty million of loans to Fiat, which is a company in Italy making automobiles that has enough exports to earn the foreign exchange to repay the loan. It has zero to do with either Italy or its government. Fiat is a private company. The second kind of loan is an infrastructure loan. Take a company in Italy like ENI, which is a government agency, that decides to build a power plant. It has projections of usage and payments and payback schedules just like any commercial company, and a loan to it has nothing to do with whether the government is good, bad, or indifferent, or any other thing. The third kind of loan in a foreign country is a loan to a U.S. subsidiary that's guaranteed by the Export-Import Bank. It has zero risk, even though it comes up in the Italy total. The fourth kind of loan is a loan to a Siemens or Hoechst subsidiary in Rome, guaranteed by the parent company in Germany. There is no Italian risk in it whatsoever. And the last kind is the so-called balance-of-payments loan to the government itself, which uses it to finance its international trade. In that case the banker is trying to evaluate whether the government's financial track record is good, bad, or indifferent.

Bankers do not take a position on the government per se, only on its record, and consequently are criticized for making loans to repressive governments, but if you look at the map of freedom in the world, about 75 percent of the world has authoritarian governments. I don't like them. I grew up in this country, and I believe in it. But banks and other companies do business with countries with whom the U.S. Government has diplomatic relations. It's a very tough problem, because if private institutions like banks are thought to be making political judgments, then they are said to be "meddling in the internal affairs of other countries." The problem is compounded by the fact that today's allies may be tomorrow's enemies. The only judgment that you can make is whether you believe the will is there to create an economic climate that will permit the repayment of the loan.

The whole process is simply a case of history repeating itself. In the absence of political restraints—and frequently in spite of them—the foreign creditor and the foreign investor have always been major sources of capital for developing countries. The United States is a prime example. Foreign capital financed both our public and our private sectors. In 1854, the Secretary of the Treasury presented a detailed statement of U.S. government and corporate securities held abroad, and according to this report almost one-half of all American debt was in foreign hands.

The Dutch floated a bond issue to help build Washington, D.C.; the Manhattan Banking Company was owned by a Welsh nobleman, the Boston Copper and Gold Mining Company was incorporated in London; the Arizona Copper Company was Scottish; and the Alabama, New Orleans, Texas and Pacific Junction Railroad was 100 percent British-owned.

As in every other developing country, the U.S. was built with borrowed money. We started borrowing abroad about the time the Pilgrims landed at Plymouth Rock, and did not get completely out of debt to foreign creditors until the First World War. As a typical developing country, we imported more than we exported year by year, and we paid the interest on one year's borrowings out of money we borrowed the next. Our exports did not begin to exceed our imports until 1873, and even then our net exports were not enough to pay the interest on our accumulated debts. We were still a borrower until well into the twentieth century.

Even today, foreign capital controls directly fourteen companies on the Fortune 500 list, and several foreign banks rank among the top fifty banks in the U.S. Two hundred years after we became a nation, I am glad to say, we are still attracting foreign capital to create American jobs.

Although the development pattern is the same, the LDCs of the eighteenth and nineteenth centuries did have one significant advantage over those of today: There were no balance-of-payments statistics in those days. No enterprising analyst could measure external debt against gross national product because GNP figures had not yet been invented. Our current tendency to take our economic blood pressure every few minutes, and then confuse short-term events for significant trends, obfuscates thought on many problems. The LDCs are no exception. Whether you consider instant statistics part of the problem or part of the solution, they are here to stay and today's LDCs have to live with them. So do bankers. There have been a lot of countries that have had problems with their balance of payments—Zaire, Argentina, Poland, Korea, Peru, Turkey, and Italy are a few examples. Tomorrow, there'll be a different set of countries on the list.

The important point is that the process is in the control of human beings and the machinery exists for solving debt problems. The International Monetary Fund is a skillful organization with which the private sector works closely. For thirty-odd years in Citibank, we've hooked our international loans to the conditions set by the IMF and the World Bank. So do most other banks. In Zaire, for example, about which everyone was distraught several years ago, the IMF worked out a settlement.

There will always be some loans that are bad news, but governments have an opportunity to work them out. One early problem we had was in Liberia, where, a number of years ago, the loan was used to build an executive mansion budgeted at one million dollars. It came in at twenty-two million, and there were unpaid suppliers all over the world. We talked President Tubman into getting assistance from the International Monetary Fund, which he did. The debt was all rescheduled and repaid. That's the real answer—that it's within the capability of men and women to put in place a program that will, in fact, make a sound debt structure.

The ability of Mexico to manage its affairs and get public underwriting on Wall Street, which it has done, stands out as a superb example of economic management under difficult conditions.

The amount of money that has gone out from the commercial banking system to developing countries has been large by previous standards. It fluctuates all the time, but most of the money goes to finance exports. One must remember that all exports in the end are financed by the people who exported them. That's why the Arabs have had to finance the export of oil by channeling their surpluses through the international financial system into loans and investments to the oil-importing countries.

In the final analysis, the only thing that finances trade is reverse trade. Nothing else is capable of doing it, and the difference is made up by capital inflow and borrowing. It's a seamless process. Banks run a sovereign risk program on every country in the world. Every quarter, they evaluate the political risks, the economic risks, the state of the economy—and cut back or increase their exposure as their judgment dictates.

For the developing country trying to produce the kind of climate that attracts private capital, the American experience should be reassuring. It demonstrates that there is nothing intrinsically wrong about carrying a large external debt and that capital can be successfully imported over a very long period of time—so long as it remains capital and it is treated as an asset and not as an enemy.

There is no mystery about the definition of capital. Every economist from Adam Smith to Karl Marx has agreed that capital is nothing but stored-up labor, either your own or someone else's. Somebody has to work hard enough to earn a wage and then exhibit enough self-denial to save some of what he or she earned. There is no other way to create it. To use Marx's phrase: "As values, all commodities are only definite masses of congealed labor time." Whether the commodity is money or goods, whether it belongs to a capitalist or a communist, makes no difference. It is valuable because somebody's labor is stored up in it, and that is what you are paying for; or what you are borrowing; or, if you are running a controlled economy, what you are trying to allocate.

If you raise the price of a commodity, what you are really doing is trying to exchange the amount of labor stored in that commodity for a larger amount of labor stored somewhere else. Neither Adam Smith nor Karl Marx would have any quarrel with that statement, but this basic fact often gets lost when we fail to define terms.

Each year's grain harvest illustrates the point. The grain bin holds the result of last year's labor. You can do one of two things with it: You can bake some bread and eat it, or you can use part of it to plant next year's crop. If you do the first, you have consumed your capital; if you do the second, you have invested it.

The problem is precisely the same for the capitalist farmer as for the commissar of agriculture. The problem for both is how much of the grain will be used for baking today's bread and how much can be saved to reproduce itself in next year's harvest. The answer determines how much people are going to be eating not only this year, but next year and the year after next. This is a hard fact of life which cannot be hidden very long by even the most ingenious and creative political oratory.

The fundamental truth that always outs at the end of the day is that political manipulation never creates wealth—it can only allocate shortages. Even then, the allocation process can only fool people for a limited period of time.

The reality of the need to work to produce capital is true under any economic system. Although individual LDCs are experimenting with a wide spectrum of economic alternatives, the majority are committed to raising their citizens' living standards by accelerating economic growth. In every instance this requires a net inflow of resources from abroad. Whether these external funds will actually speed up development depends a great deal on the use made of funds after they arrive, whether they are used as tomorrow's capital or to bake today's bread. The rate of growth of any developing country will always depend more on how it makes that decision than on the amount of funds coming in from abroad. Indeed, it will significantly influence whether or not funds will flow into a country at all.

Many LDCs are trying to modernize their agriculture, expand their manufacturing, and, in some instances, transform traditional barter societies into members of the world monetary family. At the same time their social objectives require expenditures for schools, hospitals, housing, and other building blocks of modern society.

These are all worthy goals; in fact, the effort to achieve them is the whole purpose of economic development. But if a country's policymakers ignore the need for capital to reproduce itself, if they keep converting it to current consumption, then tomorrow is never going to be better. Not only will the seed corn have been eaten, but outsiders observing this will cease sending their capital to such a society. Capital can only be attracted. It cannot be driven. This is true because there is a limited amount of capital for which there is an unlimited demand. Accordingly, capital moves toward the best blend of good return and safety that can be found somewhere in the world at any given time.

Countries that disregard these fundamentals find themselves with economies suffering chronic shortages of everything except inflation.

In the constant worldwide search to get something for nothing, some have embraced the idea that the elementary facts about capital formation might be overcome by relying solely on donors. It is proposed that loans be eliminated entirely and replaced by outright grants from governments or from international agencies such as the World Bank and the International Monetary Fund. Bothersome problems like debt service and repayment would then no longer arise. Alternatively, it is proposed that concessional loans be provided with maturity schedules so close to infinity and interest rates so close to zero as to accomplish the same result. The entire world savings is huge, growing at a rate of probably five hundred billion dollars a year or more. But it is not big enough to finance the impossible something-for-nothing dream for the simple reason that the world's people have not yet stored up enough labor to pay for it, even if people who worked hard and saved their money could be persuaded to do so.

A developing country that wants access to the private savings stream on a continuing basis has to adopt policies that reflect a clear understanding of what a bank is, what it can do, and what it cannot do.

The principal difference between a private bank and an official agency is that governments spend tax money, which they extract from the labor of their citizens, while banks are the custodians of whatever money people have left when the tax collector gets through with them. People who forgo current consumption to save money are very particular about what is done with their savings. They expect to be paid some interest and they expect to get their principal back when it is lent out. They also know that this will happen only if their money is put to the productive use of creating wealth.

In short, private banks can, and do, help developing countries create wealth, but they cannot help allocate shortages.

A significant number of developing countries have come to appreciate this fact. They have also recognized that the policies needed to maintain external creditworthiness with private banks are the very same policies needed to meet their own national development objectives.

The importance many countries attach to their external creditworthiness, and their ability to maintain it, has been demonstrated again and again. When problems do arise, and it is almost certain that they will from time to time, the adjustment process that is triggered can and does work. Countries undertake these adjustment policies with the expectation that private banks will respond positively to demands for credit from responsible borrowers. This expectation has not been disappointed.

The capacity of the international banking system is so large in relationship to the demands of the developing countries, even taken collectively, that there is no question of its ability to handle the capital flows involved. There is, however, always the question of whether public opinion in the industrialized countries, particularly the United States, will become a major constraint on the expansion of such activity because lending to developing countries is perceived by many as intrinsically too risky. A lot depends upon the public and official perception of the private banks' capability in evaluating the countries in which they have significant assets.

For the welfare of the developing countries themselves, therefore, it is essential that the private banks' credit standards not be lowered. Private banks must maintain selectivity among borrowers and be guided by the actuarial principle of spreading risk and avoiding concentration. While many developing countries are now, and will remain, creditworthy borrowers, some will not achieve that status for a long time to come. This is one reason why the available official aid funds will have to be increasingly focused on these poorer nations, and the amounts available enlarged as much as possible.

Meantime, the constant search for a new crisis swings a sharply focused but badly aimed public spotlight from topic to topic, periodically putting loans to LDCs in the limelight. A few years ago, we were assured by experts that all loans to utilities in the U.S. were shaky because when the price of fuel went up, regulatory bodies would not permit the increased costs to be passed through to customers, and few utilities could sell equities in the market. In a very few years, bankers were soliciting utility loans and Wall Street houses vied to sell their securities. In short, the adjustment process works in economics as it does in politics.

Perspective is now and always has been the best antidote for hysteria about passing problems. It is also a check upon grandiose plans that are touted from time to time as having repealed the iron laws of economics. The continuing ability of private banks to play a major role in the external financing of the developing countries will be affected significantly by how borrowers and lenders act to create a true public perspective of the risks and rewards involved in it.

The best way to allay these fears is to eliminate from our dialogue some of the unrealistic and overly political elements and get people to focus on issues that can be of true benefit to the people living in the developing countries. The details of economic development are extremely complex. The basic economic principle involved is very simple.

To look at what has gone wrong in some developing countries since 1982, we have to start at what went wrong in the rest of the world. First, there had been a worldwide recession starting in 1979, which left some thirty million people unemployed in the OECD nations; second, there was a quantum jump in the price of oil from two dollars a barrel in 1973 to thirty dollars by 1982; third, an unprecedented decline of world exports in 1979 and 1980 led to the lowest commodity prices in years. This global trauma was enough to unseat many governments, substantially alter trade flows, and drive many countries into liquidity crises.

The technical lending problem that surfaced in many less developed countries was the lack of private investment. Too much was financed by debt and too little by equity. In many countries, this state of affairs was as much a political decision as an economic one, brought on by national policies that tended to equate foreign capital with exploitation. Those countries that attracted foreign capital, and let it flow in and out without let or hindrance, did not have problems of the magnitude of those with restrictive investment policies. These policies were not put in place entirely by accident. Senator Daniel Patrick Moynihan made the point in a brilliant article in *Commentary* magazine a decade ago. What he called the "British Doctrine" was carried around the world by the students of the London School of Economics who returned home after their studies and took official positions that influenced policy in the developing world. Indeed, many of these former students became finance ministers. The Fabian Society's ideas, taught by the London School of Economics at that time, held that profit was synonymous with exploitation; that public ownership of the means of production should be substituted for private ownership; that foreign investment capital constituted an invasion of national rights; and that there was plenty of wealth to go around, if only it were fairly distributed.

As one developing country after another picked up and expanded these ideas, with local twists and turns, foreign investment was actively discouraged by myriad regulations and in some cases frozen out altogether. Without that layer of equity to absorb the massive shock of worldwide recession, projects financed entirely by debt soon got into trouble. With the blinding clarity of hindsight, bankers, along with many others, made a mistake in not recognizing the seriousness of this structural defect, which would become readily apparent at the advent of a worldwide recession. The developing countries that followed this policy of freezing out foreign capital made the mistake of assuming that more debt would always be available in world capital markets. Some western governments encouraged and applauded this "British Doctrine" for others, although not adopting it themselves. Many developed countries, my own included, made a mistake in pursuing stop-go monetary policies that drove up interest rates and helped produce the worldwide recession which caused so many social and financial strains.

As world recovery occurs, and one country after another puts in place economic policies that bring right their balance of payments, their access to markets will return, but perhaps on a somewhat different basis from before. It is reasonable to expect that access in the future will be somewhat easier for those nations that welcome a layer of investment than for those that do not. The latter will have a much more difficult time in raising from private sources, both local and foreign, the amount of money they need to keep their economies growing.

At any given time there are basically two kinds of money circulating in the world. There is money that the tax collector controls and there is money that remains in the hands of individuals after the tax collector got through with them. These two kinds of money behave in very different ways.

The kind of money that has recently passed through the hands of the tax collector will be sent wherever some government or international agency staff thinks it ought to go.

The other kind of money—the money that escaped the tax collector's net and remains in the private sector—will go only where it wants to go. It flows toward the best blend of risk and return. It can be attracted, but it cannot be pushed.

It is this second kind of money that is entrusted to the world's commercial banks. It is for this reason that comparing the loans and other assets of commercial banks to those of governments or international lending agencies is a textbook example of comparing apples to oranges. And yet this fundamental confusion is at the bottom of much of the debate about the international debt situation.

Much of what we read and hear about the role of commercial banks in international lending seems to raise the question: "What *should* be the role of private banks?"

That is the wrong question. The real question is: "What *can* be the role of private banks?" And the answer is that you may be able to pull a wagon with a piece of rope but you cannot push it. Unlike the tax collector, the commercial banker is not equipped with sticks and stones. Nor should he be.

As the pool of money made available by the tax collectors of the world has seemed to be less capable of satisfying the needs of the debtor countries, more and more arguments have been advanced that attempt to make private funds behave like public funds. It can't be done.

The second fundamental thing to be considered is that we are not living in the same world we grew up in. Since the first commercial communications satellite went up in 1964, we have been moving closer and closer to a one-world international market. The monetary and fiscal actions of governments are instantly communicated all over the world and the market's judgment shows up in the form of currency exchange rates. There is no way to hide bad policy from the millions of decision-makers that constitute the world market. Some governments have not yet grasped the full implications of the information standard and continue to believe you can fool the world market over time. Technology is against them.

An individual country may place legal or regulatory obstacles to the free flow of electrons just as it may censor its postal services or its media. But the net result will be to disadvantage its own citizens, banks, and businessmen in their efforts to compete in the one-world marketplace. Placed in this context, it is clear that international banks have not created this one-world financial marketplace; a one-world marketplace has created international banks. A government that places its own banks at a disadvantage will not succeed in changing the pattern. It will only succeed in transferring much of its banking activities to some foreign country.

Behind the speed of electronic transfers and global marketplace, banking fundamentals still apply. In fact, they have never changed. The simple fact is that while lenders can reschedule or stretch maturities, only the borrower can take the actions necessary to repay debt. If a corporation cannot earn money by selling a product in sufficient quantities at a price the market will pay, and at a profit, that company cannot repay the loan no matter how long the term is extended or how low the interest rate. There is no magic wand, no bold new plan that will solve the problem, because whether you count on your toes or use a one-megabyte microchip, two and two is still four in every language. Unlike a business corporation, a country has almost unlimited assets in its people, its government, its natural resources, its infrastructure, and its national political will. As lenders, banks can supply time for an adjustment process to work—and they do work—but they cannot put that process in place. That can only be done by the country itself. This observation is true of all governments—yours, mine, or any other. Bad economic policies can ruin any economy over time. We have all seen in our lifetime countries destroyed by inflation. Recently we saw the City of New York almost go down, but we also saw it pull itself back to economic health by the novel economic device known as balancing the budget.

Today, a few years after the scare headlines produced by some world leaders, New York City enjoys an investment-grade rating on its bonds and access to the market. There was no bold breakthrough. It was simple Benjamin Franklin economics.

Although people now love to focus on the approximately $40 billion of commercial bank interest payments on LDC debt and wonder what can be done about it, they often overlook the fact that this amount is about 11 percent of the $361 billion import bill paid by the developing countries. We all know that if the OPEC nations would drop the price of oil by ten dollars a barrel, or if countries selling manufactured goods would cut their prices and stretch out their terms, or if industrialized nations would mount massive aid programs, then no doubt things would improve for the developing countries in the short run. But in the longer run, all these measures would tend to relieve the pressure to build solid economic growth.

And so, too, would measures such as capitalizing interest on LDC debt. Whether you capitalize all future interest, or only that portion of it which exceeds a "reasonable rate" (whatever that might be), you do not cure the problem. You only hide it. The global marketplace will not be fooled. If the market perceives that a particular country prefers to issue an unlimited amount of its own interest capitalization notes, rather than do what it, and only it, can do to regain its strength and discipline, then the market will shun this paper, no matter what its rate or terms.

National governments in all countries have been debasing their currencies for more than two thousand years, and so there is very little mystery left about how they do this, or even how to stop it. We know what measures must be taken to right an economy over time. We know that the IMF has overseen dozens of successful programs and we know that the nature of these programs is similar no matter what language is spoken. They are all based on the fact that no one can do for a borrower the things it must do for itself.

There were very few at the IMF meeting in Toronto, when

the first wave of the debt crisis hit in 1982, who would have predicted how far we have come in the adjustment process. Mexico led the way, and 1983 was a year of sacrifice, adjustment, and negative growth. These programs have worked. Mexico's public sector deficit fell from 18 percent of GNP in 1982 to 8.5 percent in 1983 and still further to approximately 6.5 percent in 1984. Three years ago, Mexico's current account deficit was $13 billion and by 1983 it became a surplus of $5.5 billion, for a swing of $18 billion in two years. The trade surplus more than doubled, to $13.7 billion. All this enabled the Mexican government to raise $5 billion in new money, which was first thought by some to be impossible and then said to be too little. Out of this program, which is not without cost, growth resumed in 1984 at 2 to 3 percent, and it should accelerate to 5 or 6 percent in 1985. All this was done by a skillful financial team and a determined Mexican government. It is a pattern that can be repeated by many other countries.

The dramatic improvement in the balance of payments position of the 110 non-OPEC developing countries is another case in point. This deficit in 1981 was about $108 billion; by 1983, it was cut almost in half, to about $55 billion. This was done by the governments involved, with the help and advice of the IMF. Those that were successful went back to basics. When governments tilt the landscape, money flows may reverse direction. Commercial banks are the conduits through which much of the world's money and credit flows. It is certainly possible to dam up the conduits, but if you do, the ultimate result will be catastrophe when the dam finally breaks, as it surely will.

The most productive role our commercial banks can play in the prospective world environment is to keep the conduits open and to play our traditional role of reminding all who will listen that there are no magic solutions to problems brought on by bad monetary and fiscal policies. These problems can be cured only by a return to sound policies. These policies take time to work, and while the banks can help supply that time, only political will can put the proper programs in place. Those programs do not make headlines, but they have worked in the past and will work in the future. Benjamin Franklin, more than two hundred years ago, summed it up in two sentences: "If you know how to spend less than you get, you have the philosopher's stone. . . . Take care of the pence and the pounds will take care of themselves."

That is as true today as it was then.

If It Works, Don't Fix It

· ■ ·

Way back in the twelfth century, when Italian artisans started construction of a bell tower for the cathedral of Pisa, they had no idea their handiwork would become one of the wonders of the world. Despite the fact that the leaning tower of Pisa has stood for centuries, it is not unusual for students of structural engineering to reach a point in their studies where they can no longer gaze on it with equanimity. Although the tower of Pisa has captured the awe and admiration of generations, the students, flush with their new knowledge, are seized with a barely controllable impulse to do something about it. How could it have stood all these years? How could it have been built without their skills? Why did not some government regulator stop this precarious project?

Today, it would appear that there are some people who are seized by a similar impulse when they contemplate the smoothly functioning, admirably efficient—but unregulated—international Euromarkets, which Peter Drucker has called "a financial instrument that may have saved the world economy, and indeed the free-market system." Despite that accomplishment, the regulatory-minded see a free market teetering perilously, threatening to collapse at any moment, unless they can somehow manage to control it.

Today, there is about six hundred billion dollars in the Eurodollar market, we think. I say "we think" because no one knows how many times the dog is counted when it runs by the door. Let me give you an example. Citibank makes a placement with Barclays in London for one dollar and Barclays places it with Crédit Suisse, which places it with Société Generale, which places it with Chase Bank. How many times did the dog run by the door? Nobody really knows: the balance sheet remains exactly the same since all any of these banks get is a cable saying charge one account and credit the other. In reality, there are no dollars overseas. They are only here, because the only place anyone can spend a dollar is in the U.S. They're traded overseas, and they're payable overseas, but there never is a problem about "all those dollars abroad." If someone wished to withdraw them all one day, he could not, because the dollars cannot leave the system, which is a closed loop.

It is a paradox that this relative freedom in the international Euromarkets exists only because of various governments' efforts to restrict such freedom. The remarkably efficient Euromarkets were produced by the actions of sovereign nations—the United States prominent but by no means alone among them—to govern and restrict the flow of capital across borders.

Britain put controls on sterling, effectively withdrawing it from international markets. The so-called Regulation Q of the Federal Reserve Board, with its ceilings on interest rates; the 1963 Interest Equalization Tax, with its prohibitive effects on the purchase of American securities issued by non-Americans, which was finally repealed in 1984; and the Foreign Direct Investment Program of 1965 had all served to drive capital into the Euromarket, where interest rates are determined by the interplay of supply and demand, not subject to the passing whims of national regulators and lawmakers.

A free international market developed out of these restrictions and grew into one of the most remarkable phenomena of the postwar world. Just as free speech is feared by many governments, so also are free financial markets, because prices and costs are a kind of economic free speech that might embarrass governments. Today's free markets, like the Amsterdam bankers of the seventeenth century, put a price on national currencies that reflects buyers' judgments of national fiscal and monetary policies. This has never been well received. Many years ago, Charles de Montesquieu congratulated bankers for making it impossible for princes to secretly devalue their coinage. He observed that the function of judging the value of money would not enhance a banker's popularity with governments. Montesquieu turned out to be right on all counts—today only the vocabulary has changed. Governments now talk of "stateless money" as a term of opprobrium, and "working parties" have replaced princes to devise ways to control the market. Congress has investigated American banks to explain the weakness of the dollar from time to time, and other governments watching inflation consume the world's capital look to others to blame. But the free Euromarket, like the free press, does not create news, it only reports it.

The road to freedom is never easy and once lost is hard to regain. The benefits of free markets in ideas, politics, and money are plain for all to see. The rebirth of Europe after World War II is a clear and dramatic illustration of this effect. Europe after the war dismantled the controls and restrictions it had before. International trade barriers fell, exchange was relatively unrestricted, the climate for investment became freer and more hospitable. This relative freedom became the lever that enabled Europe's rebuilding to proceed at an astonishing pace. Output per person increased three times as rapidly as it had before the war. World trade increased 500 percent in twenty-five years. None of this was achieved without pain and effort—and much of it over the objections and warnings of those who thought only centralized planning could solve our problems.

It is the same whenever free and open trade replaces the

restrictions of selfish, protective economic systems. The efficiency of it all confounds the regulators, while the consumer enjoys the benefits.

Jean Monnet, architect of the European Coal and Steel Community, recalled the founding of the community in his memoirs: "In retrospect, it is hard to realize the effect of such a change, because the new situation now seems so normal that one can hardly imagine the absurd system it replaced."

I remember vividly the debate in Europe when it was planned to dismantle the European Payments Union—a complex government clearing system for inter-European trade. The fact that a handful of foreign exchange traders could handle the greatest two-way trade in the world—at that time between Canada and the United States—astounded the experts. But the EPU was dismantled, and the market did work. In fact, very few people even remember the EPU today.

In this era, Eurodollars have accomplished miracles that the most conscientious central planners have never dared imagine, much less approach. The most dramatic demonstration of how a free international financial market can rescue the world economy—in spite of the most vigorous efforts to prevent it—occurred in 1974. At the time, you will recall, many of the world's experts, with the notable exception of Citibank, were confidently predicting that it was hopeless to expect to recycle the tremendous surpluses generated by the Organization of Petroleum Exporting Countries, because there was no formal, regulated machinery in place to handle such a task. As it turned out, the market recycled these surpluses with very minor casualties precisely because there was no formal, regulated machinery to handle this task.

One might expect that the stellar performance of recycling sixty billion dollars of OPEC surpluses would win the plaudits of the crowd, that the experts would be delighted with a herculean task well done. No such thing happened.

The spectacle of the market working so impressively, instead of inspiring universal confidence, seemed only to fan the indignation of all those who are still determined to straighten up the tower of Pisa. Their desire to control the international financial markets as they control so many national financial markets is, however, a vain wish.

The market remains free, offering the efficient, flexible, and prompt delivery of funds where they are needed on a worldwide basis.

For the first time in world history, the LDCs have a way out of the vicious circle of poverty and the lack of development capital. The Eurocurrency and Eurobond markets are today providing thirty billion dollars a year with no political strings to creditworthy LDCs. This has enabled some of them to achieve the unthinkable, a doubling of standards of living in ten to fifteen years.

Should the regulatory fever suddenly seize the governments of the Group of Ten nations, the result would be the same as it has been in earlier cases. Some new free market would promptly spring up outside their regulatory reach. The same actions would proceed, barely missing a step. Only the venue would have changed.

There are, however, other models we can see around us. In all of our individual countries we see examples of the futility of attempting to make water run uphill. In the U.S., educational examples are frequently provided by our Department of Energy.

A few years ago, Americans were lined up at gasoline stations waiting for gas, because the Energy Department had first ordered the refining of too much heating oil instead of gasoline, then allocated the available gasoline to the wrong places.

This is the kind of wisdom and direction that many would like to see brought to the international financial markets. So far, however, world capital markets have managed systematically to adjust and preserve the world's economic balance without waiting for governments to tell them how to do it. In fact, the markets usually are well on the way to solving a problem about the time that regulators become aware of it and start gearing up to tell us how to manage it.

Members of the international banking community are the recipients of much of this gratuitous advice. Had the financial markets followed the advice of those who also devised ways to solve the oil problem, the world's financial markets in 1973 and 1974 would no doubt have performed every bit as successfully as the world's oil markets in fact did. Instead, we adhered to traditional principles of sound banking, with the result we see so clearly.

Those who predicted six years ago that the end of the world was at hand, however, are still with us, and standing by their revelation. After all, they have a heavy investment of intellectual capital to protect. Rather than changing their minds, they keep changing the date, validating Winston Churchill's observation: "Man will occasionally stumble over the truth, but most of the time he will pick himself up, and continue on."

To say that the market handled and is handling the financial recycling is not to say that the end of the era of cheap energy is no longer a serious problem to the whole world's economy. It is. To say that the market must remain free is not to say that the central banks of the world should fail to monitor with care the functioning of the market. They should. To say that the commercial banking system of the world performed extremely well in crisis is not to say that the system should not be improved and strengthened. It should. What I am saying is that in attacking our problems in the 1980s we have two models to guide us. We can learn from our experience with what has come to be called the Euromarkets, but is actually one huge international free marketplace. Or we can expand our experience with the kind of regulated markets exemplified by the U.S. Department of Energy and its counterparts around the world.

In my country, the free market and the bureaucracy furnish models of one system that works and one that doesn't. There is no mystery about it. The free market works because thousands of participants vigorously pursue what they believe to be their own self-interest, and thus rational bargains are struck between buyers and sellers. The U.S. Department of Energy model doesn't work because it attempts to substitute centralized policy judgment for the distributive wisdom of the marketplace. If all that did were to fail, the damage would be contained. But in most instances of this kind, the real casualty is individual liberty, the loss of a little bit more of our freedom of choice.

It appears that Europe is beginning to free up some markets. After more than forty years, exchange controls in the United Kingdom have been abolished, and there are signs in other countries that authorities wish to let the market function. This is a cause of great hope for the future. No one with any experience would predict that the future will be easy, that enormous problems will not be encountered, that many crises will not be faced. Against this, there is a growing awareness that if we free up the immense innovative talent of mankind, we can continue to feed ourselves and raise the world's standards of living and life expectancy, as we have done the last few decades.

There are always those to whom the future seems impossible because they discount the courage and genius of mankind. The Malthusians and their modern counterpart, the Club of Rome, are still waiting for doomsday. But there are others who are working for tomorrow. If we do not turn back from liberal free market principles into the swamp of protectionism, I, for one, have no doubt that we can advance the cause of mankind in the '80s and '90s even more than we have in the '60s and '70s.

The relatively free world of trade and finance we have been building together is eyed by many the way students of engineering eye the tower of Pisa. I would suggest to them that we listen to a bit of American backcountry wisdom, not elegant in form, but correct in substance: "If it ain't broke, don't fix it."

Agents of Change
Are Rarely Welcome

• ■ •

At the very beginning of the world, when Adam and Eve were driven from the Garden of Eden for disobedience and told that they must earn their bread henceforth by the sweat of their brows, Adam consoled Eve by saying: "We live in an age of transition." For them change was both rapid and drastic. Moreover, the physical change was accompanied by an equally great alteration in their value systems—they quickly learned to distinguish good from evil.

All history since has been dominated by change. Today, as at the beginning, change is swift and startling in the scientific and technological world, but it is the changes in our value systems that cause us the most agony. Despite protestations that innovation is welcome, mankind in general and sovereign authority and bureaucracies in particular resist change to the bitter end. Nothing upsets us more than to be told, as Abraham Lincoln once observed, that "our purposes differ from those of the Almighty." Everywhere change is popular in concept but uncomfortable in practice. The canny bureaucrat never opposes the idea of change; instead, he throws up a smokescreen of plausible reasons to abort change *now.* This rearguard action takes many forms. Specifically, whenever the times are out of joint, the serpent-devil theory of history is revived to explain away the events that have gone wrong. The first commentator on the human condition no doubt attributed society's troubles to malevolent forces. In every age since Eve was enticed by the serpent, observers have uniformly described their problems as unique, and caused by whatever passed in their time for a devil. Primitive societies, of which many still survive in modern guise, blame a bewildering array of gods for bad news. This habit of looking outward to explain trouble was placed in the early Judeo-Christian era under the broad rubric of "God's will."

Today, as always, we are in an age of transition, and as always various segments of society are moving at different speeds. The value systems of the young generally change faster than those of the aged. The scientist who split the atom finds that his disciplines have moved at a faster gait than have their counterparts in international law. The economies of the developed countries move at a pace different from those of developing lands.

A few years ago, Thomas Hughes wrote at least half seriously:

> One can say that the twentieth century is currently made up of fourteenth century farmers, fifteenth century theologians, sixteenth century politicians, seventeenth century economists, eighteenth century bureaucrats, nineteenth century generals and twenty-first century scientists.

It is not a bad analysis save for the American farmer, who belongs to the twentieth century.

Such discontinuities in world society are partly responsible for the current concern about world corporations. Those multinational companies have been blamed for everything from interfering in the political affairs of host countries to causing the revaluation of currencies by speculating on the international markets.

Yet the great global corporations of the world are now the principal agents for the peaceful transfer of technology and ideas from one part of the world to the other. Since no country has a monopoly on industrial and agricultural skills, this transfer of men, money, and ideas is necessary if we are to raise the world's living standards, but the perceptions of the needs of mankind are not uniform in the public and private sectors. As a general rule, the politicians have been engaged in fragmenting the world, while the multinational corporations have been viewing the planet as a single marketplace, and drawing peoples together in the process. The clash of these perceptions has understandably created a great deal of intellectual friction, which has been manifest in great outpourings of scholarly and not so scholarly attempts to clarify the issues between the public and the private sectors. We have witnessed lengthy debates about such weighty details as whether we should call a company multinational, transnational, international, supernational, or perhaps some other term in some other language. None of this rhetoric has been really useful. It is the kind of clarification that consists of filling in the background with so many details that the foreground sinks out of sight.

What has tended to be pushed from sight is the real nature of the choice confronting us. The arguments that use the world corporations as their focus are only a proxy for the real issue. The struggle for control of the future is not between national companies versus international, nor European companies versus American or Japanese, nor even the fashionable theme of the developed countries versus the developing, most recently styled as a north-south confrontation. The debate is really the continuation and intensification of the battle between two historic ideas concerning economic and social behavior.

One idea, associated with terms like "free trade" and "free enterprise" and "laissez-faire," holds that business is politically neutral, existing only to satisfy the economic desires of the world's people. The other, older idea holds that business is—or should be—the chosen instrument of the state; or, what amounts to the same thing, that the state should be the chosen instrument of business.

In order to draw any useful conclusions about the place of the world corporation in this dispute, it is necessary to set multinational enterprise in historical perspective. It is then possible to comprehend why our world corporations are so profoundly upsetting to so many people in and out of governments around the world.

Each of us in every country is the child of individual experience. The difficulty in communicating our value systems to one another is further complicated by the fact that the cultural histories of others do not have high priority in our national universities. In a word, we tend to be ignorant of other societies.

Despite the enormous advances in communication and the remarkable technology for instant transfer of visual images via satellite, we are still surprised and amazed when people in different parts of the world espouse value systems radically at variance with our own. It astonishes many Americans to find that some of the ideas of Colbert, the finance minister of Louis XIV, still appear to dominate a certain section of European thinking about trade and investment. The highly restrictive purchasing regulations in effect in many European countries stem from Colbert's dictum:

> All purchases must be made in France, rather than in foreign countries, even if the goods should be a little poorer and a little more expensive, because if the money does not go out of the realm, the advantage to the state is double.

In my own country, some of our Buy American laws were passed, unwittingly, under the influence of Colbert's dead hand.

To a European or to a Japanese, it is elemental that foreign trade is a country's lifeblood. Trade generates the revenue that sustains their governments. Foreign trade should inevitably be part of foreign policy. It comes as a shock to Americans, however, to discover that foreign ambassadors to the United States are helping to sell airplane engines, machine tools, or whatever their nationals need help in selling. At the same time, it is equally incomprehensible to Europeans, to Japanese, to Latin Americans, and to Africans that the United States Government takes a basically adversarial position toward business. Activities of American companies in foreign lands have long been regarded with great suspicion here at home. To Americans, foreign trade has until recently been a peripheral activity engaged in only in the event that the domestic market did not absorb our entire production. All these attitudes are deeply rooted in history and so will change only slowly. One consequence is the inherent unpopularity of the multinational corporation.

There are other, deeper roots for this hostility, however, which date back to medieval times. The first merchants, traders, and moneylenders were motivated largely by profit considerations. Feudal barons, on the other hand, looked to military power for survival and expansion. As competition between feudal rulers increased, the merchants and traders began to associate themselves with the sovereign authorities to gain commercial advantage. In return for commercial favors, they financed the wars of competing sovereigns. Merchants bankrolled the Crusades. In return they got monopoly powers to trade in large areas of the known world. The fusion of the tradesman and the royal sovereign in the sixteenth and seventeenth centuries eventually became known as mercantilism, and all external business was conducted by the chosen instruments of the state. It is not surprising, therefore, that developing countries now believe that the navy always follows the traders; if, indeed, it does not precede them. In the mercantilist world, commerce and industry were viewed as what present-day mathematicians call a zero-sum game; profit for one side inevitably meant equal loss for the other. The reality that buyer and seller could both profit from the same transaction defied mercantilist logic. The truth that business is not a poker game which transfers a static pot of money from one player to another, that instead the game creates wealth for all players, was perceived only over many years, with painful slowness.

In the mercantilist world, nations vied for overseas territories in order to control their markets. Many countries set up monopolistic trading corporations to manage trade and supply all commodities to the colonists, whether natives or settlers. There were the Dutch East India Company, the English East India Company, the French East India Company, the Hudson Bay Company and the Virginia Company. Since these companies made a profit, mercantilist dogma made it clear that exploitation of the colonists must be involved. Therefore, this practice of picking a commercial enterprise as a chosen instrument served to intensify the hostility against both the monopolistic companies and the metropolitan country that chartered them. In the American case, enmity generated by this commercial device was one of the precipitating causes of our Revolution. An excerpt from a Boston newspaper printed in 1765 summed up colonial sentiment:

> A colonist cannot make a button, a horseshoe, nor a hobnail but some sooty ironmonger or respectable buttonmaker of England shall bawl and squall that his honor's worship is most egregiously maltreated, injured, cheated and robbed by the rascally Americans.

On the other side of the world, trade as exploitation also left its imprint. The Meiji restoration, dating from 1868, marked the beginning of the modern Japanese state. But even that enlightened restoration was based broadly on the concept that Japan could not withstand hated foreign encroachments unless its society was totally reorganized as an industrial power with great military strength. Japanese hatred of foreigners was not new; it dated back two centuries to the edict of 1636, which closed Japan to all foreigners, particularly Christians. That edict also forbade Japanese ships from sailing to foreign countries, prohibited Japanese from going abroad on penalty of death, and prescribed death to any Japanese who had lived abroad and tried to return to his homeland. While much of this changed following the Meiji restoration, the concept of strong, centralized power endured.

While many peoples of the world were building centralized government structures, America's economic and political impulses developed along contrary lines. Colonial experience led Americans to be opposed to centralization of economic power in chartered companies and to centralization of political power. The separation of powers, written into our Constitution as a guarantee of political freedom, also affected economic thought. The proof of this hostility to the centralization of power is evident from the fact that our basic antitrust law bears the name of a senator whose credentials as a conservative were impeccable.

Moreover, the existence of the frontier tended for many years to influence our thinking. It was not a totally alien frontier, such as existed in the older settled parts of the world, but was merely the edge of untapped resources and an enormous land mass. Our huge continent furnished an outlet for all our goods and services. The development of those seemingly illimitable resources demanded both practical and technical innovation. Because of this heritage, many Americans even today fail to understand that America is only a subsection of the world market, and that our value system is not shared by many others. Thus the Japanese and the Europeans are hard put to comprehend what often seems the strange behavior of Americans. The arrogance of the U.S. Government's desire to export its complicated antitrust concepts around the world is properly viewed by our friends abroad with both amazement and hostility. Governments in Japan and in Europe regard their business establishments as great national assets which furnish the revenue to support increasing standards of living for their people, and for the world's people as well. It is difficult for them to understand, let alone credit, the often inherently hostile position taken by the U.S. Government toward American business.

In this country, we are acutely conscious of the mercantilist tradition in Europe and the enormous concentration of power in the *zaibatsu* complexes of Japan. Many former colonial countries see the chartered monopolies of the imperial nations as the forerunners of today's world corporations. To them, our global corporations seem to be thinly disguised, government-directed chosen instruments dedicated to the pursuit of governmental foreign policy under the guise of a commercial establishment. Bitter experience with government-chartered monopolies throughout history did little to create in many of the developing countries a welcome environment for the new worldwide economic structures that began to grow during the great postwar international expansion. Even today, the Sunday supplements love to hint darkly that the modern world corporation is really an instrument of today's nation-state. The suspicion of a modern mercantilism hangs in the air. The days of gunboat diplomacy are indeed gone. We have now come full circle in the western world to what appears to many as the successor to the chosen instrument of imperialism. Thus the world corporation is questioned, not only by the host governments but in many cases by their own governments, wherever the head office may be located, despite the enormous success of these firms in supplying the world's needs.

Part of this attack stems from the clash of historic value systems. As new philosophers, thinkers, and traders appeared on the world stage at the time of the Industrial Revolution, the idea began to dawn that man by his own efforts could improve his lot in the world. Economic growth and improvement and the betterment of social conditions seemed attainable dreams. The enunciation of the principles of free trade and the doctrines of comparative advantage by Smith, Ricardo, and others can be seen as a decisive break with the mercantilist tradition. What flowed from these new ideas was a concept of dynamic economic growth, as opposed to the old notion that profit to one was loss to the other—the zero-sum game. With this new concept came a recognition of the growing interdependence of economic units. The new emerging entrepreneurial class showed an aversion to war, and began to develop more of an adversary relationship with government. In short, the hostility was mutual.

It was against this background of changing values that the prototype world corporations first began to appear in the latter half of the nineteenth century. As far back as 1865, Germany's Friedrich Bayer built a plant in Albany, New York; the next year, Sweden's Alfred Nobel established a factory in Hamburg; and the year after that, the U.S.'s Isaac Merrit Singer opened his first overseas plant in Glasgow.

In widest historical perspective, then, commercial and political history exhibited an interplay between two basically competing value systems. The first stems from the medieval age and developed through the mercantilism of the sixteenth and seventeenth centuries into nineteenth-century imperialism, then twentieth-century totalitarianism. This was accompanied by the tradition of business as the chosen instrument of government policy. The second value system arose from the earliest merchant and financier classes of the precapitalistic era and grew through the Industrial Revolution. The entrepreneurial tradition of the capitalist, independent of government, is the basis from which grew the adversary relationship between business and the state.

Of course, as in all living things, neither system developed in a pure form. Through the period of the Second World War, there is no question that the mercantilist-imperialist tradition was dominant, though the entrepreneurial tradition, when it gained preeminence from time to time and from place to place, was responsible for much of the progress in general welfare that took place among the world's peoples.

Viewed against this background, the modern world corporation is the extension to global proportions of the business tradition that grew out of capitalism and the Industrial Revolution. It is now learning how to operate in the global marketplace. The motivating factors which drive the world corporations today are basically the same as those which drove earlier entrepreneurs. Like their predecessors, the world corporations are a new expression of the entrepreneurial thrust that thrives on the free exchange of goods, services, factors of production, technology, capital, and ideas.

Since time has proved that it is more effective to attack the carrier of an alien idea than the idea itself, the agents of change come under sustained, intensified attack.

All these criticisms overlook a fundamental point. In the tough, competitive global marketplace, it does not matter where a multinational corporation's headquarters are located. Any global company, whether based in the United States, Europe, Japan, or somewhere else, will sooner or later have to operate under the same economic and political rules that govern its international competitors. In order to stay in business, any company is compelled to get its materials for production from wherever they are available most cheaply, conduct its processing activities wherever they are most efficient, and market its goods wherever there is a demand. And all of this has to be done in compliance with a bewildering variety of laws and value systems which have been constructed by our nation-states.

It is precisely this economic necessity that makes the multinational enterprise the best instrument for assuring the most efficient, most thrifty use of the world's resources. In an era when many people express concern that those resources might be squandered, the need to make them go as far as possible and to avoid waste is an economic and human necessity. Yet efficient use of the world's resources does not generate much applause for the world corporations.

The neomercantilistic ideas have never died and still furnish ammunition for critics of multinationals, both at home and abroad. These familiar themes are articulated by some in developing countries who accuse multinational companies of milking the economies of their host countries by taking more out of them than they put in. At the same time that these charges are leveled at the world's corporations abroad, labor leaders at home aver that multinationals are exporting capital, technology, and jobs that might otherwise be used to build a domestic economy.

It is a two-front war. If the international managers prove to a host country that they are creating more wealth for it than they are taking out, this very evidence will be used against them at home. If they prove to the labor unions at home that, on balance, they are creating more jobs at home than they export, or prove to their governments that the repatriated foreign earnings are good for the home country's balance of payments, that evidence fuels the arguments of their foreign critics.

Because of their intellectual training, many of the critics are quite sincere in believing that international managers are lying when they say that everybody profits from their operations, home and host countries alike. The fundamental fact, however, is that the payrolls and jobs of the multinationals exceed profits by a factor of twenty to one. That is a hard fact. It can be ignored, as can anything by the partisan, but it cannot be argued with.

The concept of global wealth creation, however, places a great strain on even the most liberal of modern nation-states. Each ruling government is primarily concerned with optimizing conditions within its own boundaries. All countries participate to some degree in international specialization, contributing to the world economy what they can do best and most profitably. But every country at some point subordinates its possible economic advantages to considerations of military security, domestic stability, the protection of home industries or economic groups, or even national pride. Many of the developing countries, struggling to feed and educate their people, deem it more prestigious to build a steel mill than a fertilizer plant or public schools.

National governments often assert their dominance over business enterprises not only in pursuit of competitive advantage abroad but also in furtherance of domestic political policies. No country permits completely free enterprise, but controls in today's world tend to come from one of two diametrically opposed political extremes, with the freer countries positioned somewhere in the middle of the spectrum.

One type of government tends to organize its economy to favor public ownership of enterprise. It adopts policies of income redistribution, regulates consumption, maximizes central planning and government allocation of resources. At the authoritarian extreme of this system are countries like the People's Republic of China, the U.S.S.R., the nations of Eastern Europe, North Korea, Vietnam, Cambodia, and the socialist countries of Africa. The fruits of this system are written plain in the current record.

The medium-term economic consequences of such policies always involve depressed internal growth rates and can lead to extreme economic degeneration, as we saw in Nasser's Egypt, Sukarno's Indonesia, and Allende's Chile.

At the other end of the political spectrum, another group of countries pursue policies that favor private business ownership, deliberately depresses current consumption in favor of capital accumulation, permits market mechanisms rather than fiat to allocate resources, tightly controls labor unions, and generally practices social regimentation. These states tend to take a positive view of the world economy and favor policies that foster global interdependence. They usually also experience relatively strong growth rates. But very often these societies produce a serious maldistribution of income that may ultimately create an explosive social situation. If the situation deteriorates, it is not unusual to see what is euphemistically called a strong military group take over the government.

All the other national economies are strung out somewhere along the spectrum between those extremes. The most comfortable location is somewhere as close as possible to the middle, but it takes an effort to stay there. Every economic crisis creates pressure on governments to flirt with one extreme or the other, sometimes with both at the same time. There is always the temptation to solve short-term problems by exchanging them for long-term instability.

In the long run, both types of controlled economies are unstable. The progressive ruination of the economy in the one case and the social regimentation and inequitable income distribution in the other cause internal pressures for radical change. When internal pressures become irresistible, the regimes in charge may either give ground gradually or be quickly replaced. The transfers of leadership from Sukarno to Suharto in Indonesia, Nasser to Sadat in Egypt, Allende to Pinochet in Chile, and Spinola to Soares in Portugal are examples of how rapidly events occur.

No matter where a government is positioned on the political spectrum, often the public and private sectors are in conflict. This natural interplay has generated a great deal of nonsense about the relative power of multinationals and governments. The facts are clear and simple.

A multinational corporation, no matter how large, is essentially helpless in the hands of a nation-state, no matter how small. Despite overwhelming evidence of this truism, disbelief abounds. The Group of Eminent Persons appointed by the United Nations Economic and Social Council in 1972, at the instigation of the then-Communist government of Chile, investigated the relative powers of multinational companies and the sovereign states. It is not now, nor ever has been, a contest. I can give you one example from New York City, where I live right next door to the United Nations headquarters.

New York, as you may know, is a hard place to park an automobile. Members of missions assigned to the UN enjoy diplomatic immunity. They can, if they choose, ignore the No Parking signs, which many of them do, to the constant irritation of less privileged New Yorkers. If I park my car in my neighborhood, the Police Department tows it away. The head of every global company is in the same fix.

There you see the true difference between sovereignty and the lack of it. If the example I chose seems a little simplistic, it is no more so than books with titles like *Sovereignty at Bay*. Or for that matter, some of the reports that were turned out by the Group of Eminent Persons who parked their cars with impunity outside my apartment house in clear defiance of local laws.

As a last resort, all any multinational company can do in its relations with a sovereign state is to make an appeal to reason. If that fails, capital, both human and material, will leave for countries where it is more welcome. Since men and money in the long run go where they are wanted and stay where they are well treated, capital can be attracted but not driven.

In the long run, it all comes down to this: the future of a global company in any one area will be determined by the degree to which a particular government is willing and able to put the material well-being of its citizens ahead of out-moded political, protectionist, or other local narrow interests. Everything discussed thus far will be resolved almost automat-ically when our nation-states make up their minds concerning that basic question.

The reality of a global marketplace has been the driving force pushing us along the path of developing a rational world economy. Progress that has been made owes almost nothing to political imagination. It has been the managers of the multi-national corporations who have seen the world whole and moved to supply mankind's needs as efficiently as politics would allow. The thousands of jobs and products that have helped raise the living standards of mankind have made this economic process highly visible to millions of people. Far too many of the world's people have now seen what the global shopping center holds in store for them. They will not easily accept having the doors slammed shut by nationalism.

The development of the truly multinational organization has produced a group of managers of many nationalities who really believe in one world. They know that there can be no truly profitable markets where poverty is the rule of life. They are a group that recognizes no distinction because of color or sex, since they understand with the clarity born of experience that talent is the commodity in shortest supply in the world. They are managers who are against the partitioning of the world, not only on a political or theoretical basis but on the pragmatic ground that the planet has become too small, that our fates have become too interwoven one with another for us to engage in the old nationalistic games which have so long diluted the talent, misused the resources, and dissipated the energy of mankind.

They realize that the engine that drives the growth of nations gives humanity the wherewithal to deal with the wretchedness of the human condition. They have learned that the multinational corporation can function amid diverse value systems, though like all instruments of progress it must move in a resisting medium.

Woodrow Wilson proclaimed a league of free nations—but the League of Nations did not survive. Wendell Willkie argued, correctly, that we have one world, a fact that the astronauts vividly proved. Nevertheless, the politicians of the world will not act. The political problems of the United Nations are a stark manifestation. The divisiveness of the European Economic Community is further evidence. Despite all our advances, the world is still socially fragmented and the incompatibility of the world's value systems has always been and still remains a cause of potential conflict. History is replete with the tragedies wrought by the efforts of one society to impose its concepts upon others.

Agents of change involve new ideas and values. They have never been welcome in any society. This is especially true when the carrier of new or strange values is, or is thought to be, alien to the society that is affected. Often the most effective way to resist change is by identifying the carrier of the new values as foreign. The word for "foreigner," from the Golden Age of Greece right up to the Middle Ages, was "barbarian." Anyone who spoke a foreign language, dressed differently, adhered to different customs and mores, was automatically considered a barbarian. "Stranger" and "foreigner" have thus from time immemorial been pejorative terms, and often synonymous with "enemy."

It should not surprise us, therefore, that the world corporation is sometimes unwelcome even though it is the carrier of technology, which is the best hope of closing the gap between the very rich and the very poor. It is often unwelcome because it is perhaps the most effective instrument by which value systems are transferred from one part of the world to another.

Mere physical change, manifested by a new factory, a new building, or a piece of complex machinery generally does not arouse the passions of the populace. But when the change moves into the realm of ideas, a wholly different and more massive impact upon society follows. If, for example, a world corporation introduces the idea of upward mobility based only on merit and not on status, this may well offend an establishment fighting to preserve its privileges.

The nature of the value systems that are carried by world corporations, as agents of change, runs the gamut from simple improvements, like better lighting in manufacturing plants, to renovating whole neighborhoods. For example, Park Avenue in New York City north of Grand Central Station used to be lined on both sides with old apartment houses. It was not until a British-based multinational corporation, Unilever, saw the potential of putting a modern office building in this area that a whole new development was sparked in my city, and opened in time new opportunities elsewhere. Today, a certain portion of the pensions received by retired employees of the British Post Office come from rents on the Merchandise Mart in Chicago, which they own.

Old ideas die hard; yesterday's liberals, who feel that central, national control is the answer to everything, are still in control of many intellectual circles. They all labor under an old illusion, which John Gardner once put as follows: "Those who seek to bring societies down always dream that after the blood bath *they* will be calling the tune." That outworn doctrine of the controlled economy—a relic of mercantilism—is becoming more and more a manifestation of the persistence of illusion over reality.

Gresham Revisited

■ ■ ■

Sitting in my office one day, attempting to collect my thoughts, I caught the eye of Sir Thomas Gresham, whose portrait hangs over my desk. It seemed to me that Sir Thomas was trying to tell us something. Gresham's law, expressed in but five words—bad money drives out good—reminds us all that money has no value except that of scarcity, which is a good compass point to keep in mind when sailing through the verbal storms of both the new and the old economics.

In addition to understanding clearly the problems of the domestic money supply, Sir Thomas was also one of the first realists on the subject of manipulation of foreign exchange rates. He wrote to his sovereign, Edward VI, as follows:

> I did raise the Exchange from sixteen to twenty-three shillings, whereby all foreign commodities and ours grew cheap; and thereby robbed all Christendom of their fine gold and fine silver. And by raising of the Exchange, and so keeping of it up, the fine gold and fine silver remains forever within our realm.—Sir, if you will enter upon this matter, you may in no way

relent, by no persuasion of the merchants. Whereby you may keep them in fear and in good order: for otherwise if they get the bridle, you shall never rule them.

Here, in short, is realism of a very high order. For what Gresham did in a few blunt words was to pinpoint the intimate connection between international trade, monetary fluctuations, and nationalistic considerations.

We have a tendency today, in considering our modern-day global economic problems, to treat each of those factors in isolation, when in fact they are still very much connected. We get frequent reminders.

In the late 1970s, under the Carter administration, the dollar was periodically battered on the foreign exchange markets because foreign traders did not see any consistent economic policy coming out of Washington. One member of the Federal Reserve board would say, "We're going to pump up the money supply if there's any slowing of the economy," and other governors would avow that such action would not attenuate inflation. The result was that traders sold the dollar and moved into what they perceived to be harder currency. The swings got to be so great that the Federal Reserve put together a package to go in at the margin to stabilize the dollar, and it worked out pretty well. The blame, of course, was laid on the foreign exchange traders, just as a decade or so earlier a chancellor of the exchequer invented the Gnomes of Zurich to explain Great Britain's economic vicissitudes.

This situation about the futility of controls is not new. It was explained to Samuel Pepys in 1664. On January 27–29, Pepys recorded a conversation with a Mr. Slingsby about the mint and coinage of money.

> . . . he made me fully understand that the old law of prohibiting bullion to be exported, is, and ever was a folly and an injury, rather than good. Arguing thus, that if the exportations exceed importations, then the

balance must be brought home in money, which, when our merchants know cannot be carried out again, they will forbear to bring home in money, but let it lie abroad for trade, or keepe in foreign banks: or if our importations exceed our exportations, then, to keepe credit, the merchants will and must find ways of carrying out money by stealth, which is a most easy thing to do, and is every where done; and therefore the law against it signifies nothing in the world. Besides, that it is seen, that where money is free, there is great plenty; where it is restrained, as here, there is a great want, as in Spayne.

Samuel Pepys described Mr. Slingsby as "a very ingenious person," and I have to agree. Nothing much has changed except the method of moving money. Governments still attempt capital controls, often in an attempt to hold an exchange rate for its currency that the rest of the world regards as unrealistic. The difference is that such efforts now fail sooner rather than later.

My experience around the world, and I've been making the circuit for thirty years or more, is that whenever countries have poor fiscal and monetary policies, and their currency starts to depreciate, they look for an answer other than themselves. The Gnomes of Zurich disappeared from public view when they outlived their usefulness. To blame the foreign exchange traders now is like saying that the government bond market declined on Wall Street yesterday because Salomon Brothers doesn't like the U.S. Government. The fact is that the foreign exchange market now amounts to around fifty trillion dollars a year and is just too big for any one entity to move. If you took all the capital of all the banks in the United States and sold it in the foreign exchange market, it would amount to about ten minutes of trading. The myth that somebody can influence a market of that size is exactly that. No greater evidence exists than that provided a few years back when the British were fighting to keep the pound from being devalued. They lost their entire reserves and borrowed a billion dollars from the International Monetary Fund, and lost that too, all within a couple of months. They devalued the pound anyway. It was only when the IMF put Britain on a sound monetary policy that the pound began to improve. The market is just too big for even the central banks to do anything about it, as witness the failure of fixed exchange rates and the failure of the snake in Europe, and the success of floating exchange rates. In the global marketplace now, the value of the dollar at the end of the day—or that of any currency in our interdependent world—rests on the productive capacity of the issuer and how the rest of the world views the use or misuse of that capacity.

In the short term, sometimes countries or companies get into trouble with imports because they refuse to look at the real world. We lost the shoe business in New York not because of price but because of styling. The Europeans, particularly the Italians, beat us blind on styling. The international division of labor is always operative and has taken on the added dimension of consumer preference, which requires a new kind of capital.

In the United States, the sluggishness of capital formation, resulting from decades of shortsighted tax policy, has had a harsh impact on the competitive position of our older industries, for all of the reasons by now familiar and one less so.

To my mind, at least, the purpose of capital is to put in place the various tools that will permit our societies to increase their productivity. The productivity of manual workers is very largely related to the efficiency of the machines they operate. While this appears to be self-evident, not too many people have taken the second step in the thought process. This point was made most cogently by Peter Drucker when he said:

A little reflection will show that the rate of capital formation, to which economists give so much attention, is a secondary factor. Someone must plan and design the equipment—a conceptual, theoretical, and analytical task—before it can be installed and used. The basic factor in an economy's development must be the rate of brain formation, the rate at which a country produces people with imagination and vision, education, and theoretical and analytical skills.

The capital problems of the '80s can be divided into two categories: money capital and intellectual capital. The money needs of industry are generally reflected by numbers that appear to be finite even though the underlying input is often at best an educated guess.

A few examples illustrate the point. In 1948, the Pennsylvania Turnpike, the grandfather of major American toll roads, floated a bond issue of $135 million. That year government and private borrowers raised a grand total of $14 billion in American capital markets. If some study group had forecast in 1948 that toll road construction would require $3.5 billion over the next eight years, certainly the specter of a capital shortage would have reared its head. But by the time the roads were built, the size of the capital markets more than doubled. Similarly, in the mid-1950s, when the capital markets provided an average of about $30 billion, the computer industry and the airlines, to name just two, did not figure prominently in any widely publicized list for capital investment. Yet the airlines raised more than $7 billion and the computer industry more than $2 billion through underwriters in the U.S. capital markets in the 1960s. In those industries, where technology was advanced and where productivity was relatively high, capital investment grew rapidly and their competitive positions in world markets became dominant. On the other hand, when technology failed to produce sufficient increases in the rate on capital, investment dried up and some industries found themselves under pressure from imported products in their home markets.

This is another way of saying that superior intellectual capital always attracts the necessary financial capital over time because it produces a sufficiently attractive real rate of return.

The projected capital gap as such, which we hear so much about from time to time, is a misconception built on a fallacy. Everyone, whether in business, government, or academe, or even in our individual private lives, makes a list of aspirations, which then are formalized through elaborate rationales into projects with price tags on them. In that way we convince ourselves that we "need" whatever is involved and that dire consequences will occur if we do not fulfill that "need." The aggregate total of all those project lists always exceeds our resources by a wide margin. It makes a wonderful thing for clever people to write about, but those who employ the erroneous shopping-list approach to establishing a capital shortage may unwittingly invite an equally erroneous solution—capital allocation by government. Only a free market can efficiently and equitably allocate credit and capital. The so-called shortfall in capital, produced by comparing projected capital formation with our hopes and dreams, will be resolved in the same way it has always been resolved: that is, by canceling or reducing those capital investments which cannot economically be justified.

As some capital investments terminate and others take their place, our living standards and life styles are shaped differently from what we might expect, or they might fail to rise to the expectations of business, government, and consumers. But the failure of living standards to rise to our expectations will be determined not as much by the *quantity* of capital formation as by the *quality* of capital formation.

Since business and finance need a constant injection of new capital investment, the reasoning runs that increased capital investment means more production, if all other things remain equal. More goods and services would relieve shortages, and thus ease prices and drive down the rate of inflation. That scenario has a natural logic which commends it, but the hooker is in the qualifying phrase, "if all other things remain equal." Since most things in this world are comparative, it becomes pertinent to point out the higher investment being made by other industrial countries. When we look around the world, comparative totals of gross investment as a percentage of GNP put the U.S. at the bottom of the list with a rate of 18.2 percent. Japan was at the top with 36 percent, then France with 28 percent, and Germany with 26 percent. Unfortunately, these higher investment rates did not produce lower inflation. The fact was that Japan, the country with the highest rate of investment, also had the highest rate of inflation. France, with the next-highest rate of investment, produced the next-highest rate of inflation. As we reflect upon these numbers, it becomes unfortunately clear that there is nothing in the relationship between levels of investment and inflation in this country or abroad to suggest that higher levels of capital formation—desirable as that goal must be—will save any nation from inflation. Only governments create inflation and only governments can solve it. Similarly, governments now must face the new realities of international trade.

Although political ideology remains a disruptive force, many nations now recognize that self-interest and the common interest are not mutually exclusive. Instead of turning inward and building walls, developed and developing nations that have welcomed foreign trade and investment have been able to speed social as well as economic progress.

The Soviet Union, for example, which once closed itself off from the markets of the West, has become one of the largest markets in the world for advanced technology. Some Eastern European countries have long understood the importance of foreign goods and capital for their development. Funds from the West have supported an assortment of projects in Eastern Europe.

Anyone who has observed the gyrations of our global economy since the end of World War II cannot fail to be impressed by the spectacular growth of countries like Brazil. Credit for Brazil's progress and prosperity is due most of all to its willingness to rely on incentives rather than directives to attract foreign investors. Brazil's enlightened investment policies have made that country the largest recipient of development loans from the World Bank, and lured billions in direct investment from abroad. There is, perhaps, no better expression of world confidence in Brazil's future than the fact that roughly half the funds committed in that country are reinvested each year.

Although the tragic events in Southeast Asia overshadowed the region's economic picture, several nations there have been showcases for the effective encouragement of capital investment. Singapore is a stunning example of the advantages of being hospitable to foreign capital. At the beginning of 1960, the local economy depended almost entirely on services and Singapore's role as a distribution center. A decade later, the mangrove swamps were transformed into a modern industrial center, thanks to government-backed investment incentives.

Singapore, along with some of its neighbors, has adopted a sensible approach to the repatriation of funds. In general, there are no restrictions on full remittance of profits and capital, and in addition, there are tax holidays and tariff incentives. Singapore itself is essentially a free port, since goods can move in and out of the island as freely as money.

The booming economy of Singapore serves to illustrate and underscore the direct correlation that invariably exists between prosperity and economic freedom. West Germany, one of the most affluent of all nations, has had a minimum of restrictions on trade, as have Belgium and Switzerland. Both Japan and France have become less restrictive in order to create a more cordial climate for their own goods abroad.

There is no question, of course, that when inflation is rampant and countries are plagued by unemployment and an assortment of internal ills, there is always a temptation to institute controls to obtain short-term advantage. Protectionism in a variety of guises remains a real and constant threat. The history of the world, though, confirms again and again that not only do controls fail, but, on their way to failure, they distort the global marketplace—discouraging producers, causing shortages, and creating uncertainty.

The Smoot-Hawley tariff, which touched off a tidal wave of retaliation to deepen the global depression in the '30s, is a case in point. So are wage and price controls, which have been tried and found wanting since the time of the Roman Empire. Nevertheless, the exponents of protectionism and the advocates of expropriation remain alive and well. The emergence of the Burke-Hartke Bill in the U.S. in the mid-1970s, and certain other ill-fated proposals that come before the Congress from time to time to discourage foreign investment in the United States, are classic examples of such retrogressive thinking.

The World Bank has documented clearly the fact that if someone gains a dollar from protection, someone else in the same country loses a lot more. For every $20,000-a-year job in the Swedish shipyards, Swedish taxpayers pay an estimated $50,000 annual subsidy. Protection costs Canadian consumers $500 million a year to provide an additional $135 million of wages in the clothing industry. When Japanese consumers pay eight times the world price of beef, Japanese farmers are not made eight times better off. It costs them that much more to produce it. Moreover, protectionism slows economic recovery. Slow growth, the World Bank said, is less likely if protectionism is avoided, since protection itself would reduce the incentives that promote technological innovation and improvements in productivity.

The U.S. economy is becoming more and more dependent on foreign trade, exporting 20 percent of its manufactured goods and 40 percent of its agricultural produce. Foreign trade accounts for a third of all corporate profits and 16 percent of our country's factory jobs.

But this has not stopped the United States from seeking to curb imports of textiles, sugar, European steel, and Japanese automobiles. The U.S. Congress periodically considers legislation that would require virtually all automobiles in the United States to be built substantially of parts made in the United States.

Protectionism at best can only delay the inevitable; it can't stop change. Arthur Dunkel, the director-general of the General Agreement on Tariffs and Trade (GATT), recently used the textile industries of Europe as an example of what protectionism has achieved. Since 1977, European textiles have enjoyed more protection from so-called low-cost imports than ever before. Yet in the following three years, many European countries saw textile business failures, mill closures, and job losses at unprecedented levels. Dunkel concluded that the long struggle to preserve jobs in textiles has in many cases merely postponed their loss to a period when alternative employment is even more difficult to find.

Service industries are also facing new protectionist barriers. The reason is simple. World trade in services is now well over $600 billion a year. In many countries, a large portion of the gross national product, and consequently jobs, depend on the services sector of their economies. Barriers are most conspicuous in transportation, communications, and financial services.

For example, no operating license has been given to a foreign insurance company in Norway in four decades. Foreign engineers pay higher income taxes in Brazil than native-born engineers. London's *Financial Times* is printed in Germany and then flown to London by air freight, because of restrictions on the transmission of foreign data bases and typesetting files. Nor can the *Financial Times* use the quiet hours on other people's leased lines, because of the British Post Office's restrictions on sharing leased lines. And the United States bars foreign shipping companies from competing for American coastal trade. All together, there are more than a thousand such barriers to international trade in services. Freely competing amidst change has never been easy. We are traveling in a political direction for services that is the fundamental equivalent of high tariffs on merchandise.

Those who call for a return to the jungle of protectionist controls forget that money is fungible. When government bureaucracy restricts or restrains it, capital takes flight. For example, Washington's efforts to attenuate the importance of

Wall Street with the passing of the now defunct equalization tax merely served to exile American capital. American ceilings on interest rates merely served to develop and to fuel the Eurodollar market. This market, the creation of entrepreneurs —not politicians—has financed the great burst of trade and investment in modern history. Its success confirms beyond all doubt that in a mobile world—with an infinite demand for funds—controls are no match for market forces.

Those who oppose the free flow of capital also invariably exaggerate the power of capital. They assume that money alone can take over a company or a country. This simplistic view overlooks the fact that nation-states are governed, not by capital, but by people, by laws, and by the powerful forces of the market. If a foreign investor does not operate in the public interest, abide by the laws, and produce what people want, he will fail as others before him have failed.

Underestimating the sensitivity of capital and overestimating the power of capital indicate a lack of historic perspective. It should be obvious to those who look back into history that each nation on earth whose citizens have succeeded in bettering their lot in life has drawn heavily on the capital, experience, and expertise of others. In the end, each nation develops a unique system of its own. No two national structures are the same, nor should they be, for each, if it is to endure, must fit the temperament and the value systems of its people.

Since the early decades of American independence, the United States sought European capital to build its roads, canals, and railroads. What passed for our central bank in those days was owned and controlled by European investors. Our first Secretary of the Treasury, Alexander Hamilton, summed up the American attitude toward foreign capital in 1791 when he said:

Instead of being viewed as a rival, it ought to be considered as a most valuable auxiliary, conducing to put in motion a greater quantity of productive labor . . . than could exist without it.

Hamilton's view is perhaps more apt today than it was then. The planet has now become too small, and the fate of all of us too interwoven, to engage in nationalistic games that set nation against nation. Economic chauvinism is obsolete in a world where the prosperity of all nations depends more and more on cooperation and free trade.

The emergence of protectionist sentiments around the world is once again looming as a clear and present danger. Recently, Wilhelm Haferkamp warned that the "protectionism that kept millions on the dole forty years ago is now being presented in a new guise, with seductive, modern, rational-sounding slogans." He is right, and there is no better example of the use of cosmetic language to disguise protectionism than the slogan "organized free trade." Like organized freedom, it is an Orwellian euphemism.

The strongly protectionist tone of some recent pronouncements on trade can be traced to the emergence of certain political and economic trends in developed and developing nations. There is, for example, a sluggishness of demand in the capital equipment areas of many industrialized countries. Slow growth has been accompanied by persistent high rates of unemployment. While conventional wisdom suggests that high unemployment and free trade are traditional enemies, history does not validate this assertion. The Reciprocal Trade Act of the United States, which pushed the world community toward freer trade, was passed by our Congress in 1936, when we had massive unemployment.

This time around, we have some new factors. A number of countries in Latin America and the Far East, now in the takeoff or miracle stage of their development, are pressing their exports upon the world. Low wages and a large and productive work force have enabled these nations to excel in the production of textiles, clothing, electronics, and other labor-intensive goods. As a result, their export industries have a strong advantage in European and American markets.

Unless these countries can continue to expand their exports of manufactured goods, their economic development will be stunted and the demand for foreign assistance will be accelerated. As they expand their exports, however, important and painful shifts in the industrial structure in the United States and Europe result.

We are all aware that real wages in much of the industrialized world have risen too fast. We recognize that the wage differentials have narrowed between modern, efficient industries and older, less efficient ones. Trade restrictions which coddle inefficiency invariably lead to economic stagnation.

What is needed is a readjustment of the structure of industry in many leading countries in order to respond to competition from new arrivals on the world industrial scene. It is the tendency of governments, however, to resist such adjustments and push them off on foreigners.

While all of these problems can never be solved to perfection, they can be coped with so as to do as little damage as possible to the general welfare. What the world needs are new trading rules to deal with new competitive realities. There is urgent need for more adjustment assistance and *temporary* marketing agreements under GATT supervision to prevent what has been called guerrilla warfare in trade form erupting into open hostilities. The planet has become too small, and the fate of all of us too interwoven, for us to engage in those old nationalistic games, which dilute the talent and dissipate the resources of mankind.

Our global society is, as always, in a period of transition. The old notion that exports are good and imports are bad is being replaced by the idea that exports are the price we pay for trade and imports are the benefits we receive from it. The eternal conflict between what people pay to buy goods and what they earn to produce goods will never be easily resolved. The simple truth, however, is that to the degree we cut our imports, we are increasing costs to the consumer and inviting retaliation, for the only way the world can sell more abroad is to buy more abroad.

One intellectual discipline can borrow from another. The work in theoretical chemistry by the Belgian Nobel laureate

Dr. Ilya Prigogine has parallels in political philosophy. He has established that life can come into being and, contrary to the second law of thermodynamics, continue to expend energy without drifting into chaos or being entirely dissipated. Dr. Prigogine has explained his complex theory for laymen with an analogy of two towns—one, the walled city of feudal days, totally isolated from its surroundings, and the other in constant communication and interchange of goods, services, and ideas with its neighbors. The first city, representing the closed system of classical physics and chemistry, must inevitably decay and cease to function, while the second city, interacting with its surroundings and nourished by others, will, even as it gets more complex, become better organized, grow, and flourish.

The Prigogine parable, in my view, is equally applicable to nations. Those nations shortsighted enough to persist in raising protectionist walls against the ideas, goods, and capital of their more productive neighbors will over time share the fate of the walled city.

The conflict between protectionism and free trade is not of recent vintage. Indeed, it goes back to Biblical times, with Joseph's attempt to restrict the sale of grain in Egypt.

More than a century ago, the French economist Frédéric Bastiat drew up a petition claiming that French manufacturers of candles, lamps, and other lighting devices were suffering from the "intolerable competition" of a foreign rival. This rival, he wrote, was "in a condition so far superior to our own for the production of light, that he absolutely inundates our national market with it at a price fabulously reduced." The rival Bastiat had in mind was none other than the sun.

He went on to urge the candlemakers to challenge the competitive advantage of the sun. The sun's monopoly could be destroyed and a demand for artificial light created, he argued, by simply passing a law ordering the shutting of all windows, skylights, and other openings.

Bastiat concluded his petition, however, with this admonition:

Make your choice, but be logical; for as long as you exclude, as you do, iron, corn and foreign fabrics, in proportion as their prices approximate zero, what inconsistency it would be to admit the light of the sun, the price of which is already at zero during the day.

Bastiat's satire on the fallacy of the extreme protectionist position is as pertinent today as it was then. Yet many men are as reluctant to accept the idea of the interdependence of nations in the global marketplace as they once were to accept the Copernican theory that the sun is the center of our universe.

Man's hesitancy to adopt new concepts intellectually and adjust to them emotionally is still the greatest obstacle of all to peace and prosperity on this planet. However, those of us who do not fear change and are able to view the entire world as a market for goods, services, and ideas now have as our allies the young men and women who know that a global economy is emerging and it makes no more sense for nations to turn inward than for the French candlemakers of the nineteenth century to try to shut out the light of the sun.

EPILOGUE

· ■ ·

Risk Is a Four-Letter Word

· ■ ·

The men and women who founded our country were at once adventurers who took personal risks of the most extreme kind and pragmatists who wrote a Constitution based on the tested theory that men are not gods. No assumptions were made that elected leaders would all be selfless persons devoted to the public interest. Rather, the rock on which our structure rests is a Constitution that diffuses power, lest one person or group grow too powerful. Alexander Hamilton put it succinctly when he said: "If men were angels no government would be necessary." The system they devised based on this assumption about human nature has stood the test of time. Our government has proved to be one of the most enduring in history.

While the constitutional framework set limits on power, the driving force of our society is the conviction that risk-taking and individual responsibility are the ways to advance our mutual fortunes. Our Founding Fathers were themselves political adventurers who did not hesitate to sign a document pledging "our lives, our fortunes, and our sacred honor" in pursuit of a brighter future against overwhelming odds. They would have been more than a little surprised to learn that what they were really fighting for was a totally predictable, risk-free society.

Today, however, the idea is abroad in the land that the descendants of these bold adventurers should all be sheltered from risk and uncertainty as part of our national heritage. We seem to have raised a generation of advocates, writers, and bureaucrats to whom the word "risk" is an acceptable term only when used in connection with promoting a state lottery. Emerson's counsel—"always do what you are afraid to do"— is now rejected as too upsetting, and one should steer the safe, noncontroversial course. One has only to look at the gray stagnation of planned societies where this idea is far advanced to wonder how such a system can continue to attract so much intellectual support. But it does.

It can be argued that if the desire to avoid risk above all else becomes the predominant objective of American society, it may in the end destroy not only our economic system but our form of government along with it. At bottom, democracy itself rests on an act of faith, on a belief in individual responsibility and the superiority of the free marketplace, both intellectual and economic, over anything that might be devised for us by a committee of bureaucrats disguised as guardian angels. There is real reason to fear that those who do not share that faith have, in their efforts to build a risk-free society, not only drained the spirit of our people but already seriously impaired the viability of the most productive economic system the world has ever seen.

This is a relatively new problem for Americans. The whole of this country was opened up by people who were—no less than the Founding Fathers—at once adventurers and patriots. My grandmother, in company with hundreds more, went west in a Conestoga wagon that by today's standards was unsafe at any speed. The environmental problems were enormous. They used buffalo dung to fuel their campfires. Half of the wagon train in which my grandmother traveled was massacred by Indians. But many more followed in their tracks along trails that no government agency today, at a city, state, or federal level, would think of certifying as safe for travelers. In fact, the pioneers would probably not even be allowed to settle down at the end of their journey. The sparkling, exciting city of San Francisco was built on a set of hills that could test the footing of a mountain goat. If that were not bad enough, it lies along the San Andreas earthquake fault, which has already destroyed it once. No modern urban planner could possibly approve the building of San Francisco today. The risk would be considered too great.

The unremitting atmosphere of protective custody which now seems to surround us is producing a new kind of national mood. The American spirit of optimism and enterprise is being overwhelmed by a malaise that was best described by the English journalist Henry Fairlie, who wrote:

> If the American people for the first time no longer believe that life will be better for their children, it is at least in part because they are beginning to think that there will be no food which their children will be able to eat without dying like rats of cancer, no form of transport that will be considered safe enough to get them from here to there, and in fact nothing that their children may safely do except sit like Narcissus by a river bank and gaze at their wan and delicate forms as they throw the last speck of Granola to the fish.

This is a far cry from the spirit of enterprise that turned a raw continent into a great nation. Of course, there have always been those among us who bewail all forms of risk: political, economic, or personal. They are the ones who have never understood the Biblical injunction "For whosoever will save his life shall lose it." But in those days people of little faith did not have a nationwide, instant electronic forum for their timid views, or the power to enforce them upon others.

This growing thirst for an impossible physical and economic security has a direct bearing on whether or not we will maintain our spiritual and political freedom. The relevance of risk to liberty is direct and clear. For in the end, it always turns out that the only way to avoid risk is to leap into the arms of an all-knowing government. George Gilder put it best when he wrote that "risk and uncertainty are seen to be the problem, and government the solution in the fail-safe quest for a managed economy of steady and predictable long-term growth."

If you carry this logic to its bitter end, it all gets reduced to the motto under the picture of Mussolini that was plastered throughout Italy at the height of his power. It said: "He Will Decide." The responsibility no longer belonged to the individual. The leader would decide.

The pattern is always the same. A bureaucracy is put in place to coerce the people into doing something for "their own good." The bureaucracy then assumes a life of its own and the coercion continues as the bureaucracy's primary task long after the original purpose has been forgotten.

The Securities and Exchange Commission was created in response to a felt need to protect the investor against fraud. It was a worthy objective, but little by little its role was expanded until it attempted to dictate everything, from how a board of directors should govern a company to how lawyers should exercise their professional judgment. That kind of excess of zeal is not new. The ultimate in what now seems to be the trend in corporate governance was achieved by the City Bank of New York in 1844 when it had nine employees and fifteen directors who assisted in the day-to-day operations. If today's Citibank is obliged to revive that ratio, it is going to end up with one hundred thousand directors for its sixty-three thousand employees.

Our American economic system, like our political system, is untidy—it offends those people who love tidy, predictable societies. We make a lot of mistakes in this country, we have a lot of failures. Some people see only the failures; they cannot seem to grasp the fact that the failures are the price we pay for the successes. It's as though they wanted to have "up" without "down," or "hot" without "cold."

We read in our newspapers, and even in our business magazines, solemn words about "risky investments" and "risky loans," from writers who do not seem to realize that these phrases are as redundant as talking about a one-story bungalow. All investments and all loans are risky because they are based on educated guesses about the future, rather than certain knowledge of what will happen. Despite the most sophisticated market research, no one really knows if the public will buy a product or use a service that we are about to produce. The result might be a failure like the Edsel, with a four-hundred-million-dollar price tag, or it might be Peter Goldmark's long-playing record, which is in almost everyone's home. It could be the decision of a Joe Wilson, risking all the resources of his small company to make a copier later called Xerox, and doing it in the face of a careful study which showed that it would be a bad substitute for the familiar carbon paper.

The odds against success of any kind in our society are formidable. Some three hundred thousand businesses are started each year in the United States and only one-third of them survive as long as five years. Proponents of a safe, stagnant, boring tomorrow view this as a wasteful process, to say nothing of its being irrational. On the contrary, it is the secret of economic growth, because no one knows which venture in an endless stream of innovation and enterprise will succeed.

Our Founding Fathers understood this principle. Their industrial policy was simple and straightforward. It was to promote entrepreneurship by federally granted patents, or in the words of the Constitution: "The Congress shall have the power to promote the progress of science and useful arts by securing for . . . authors and inventors the exclusive right to their respective writings and discoveries."

They were motivated by the notion that people who do creative work should be rewarded for it—because it would encourage creativity. This section of the Constitution was put into practice by the act of 1790 that created a patent board, consisting of the Secretary of State, the Secretary of War, and the Attorney General. It was a prestigious group: Thomas Jefferson, Henry Knox, and Edmund Randolph. As he watched the flow of ideas, Jefferson later said, the patent law gave "a spring to invention beyond my conception."

Abraham Lincoln, who himself obtained a patent, later observed that "the patent system added the fuel of interest to the fire of genius."

Our government servants who administered the Patent Office did not always have the vision of the entrepreneurs who burdened them with new ideas. Henry Ellsworth, the commissioner of patents in 1844, opined that the flood of inventions seemed "to presage the arrival of that period when further improvements must end." Later, a director of the Patent Office urged President McKinley to abolish the office, since "everything that can be invented has been invented."

Since the first patent was granted on July 31, 1790, to one Samuel Hopkins for a method of making Pot Ashes, well over four million patents have been granted.

Although I cannot build a model for you today within a twelve-inch square, as used to be required, I would submit that we have before us a living model of a perpetual-motion machine in America, and that those who learn how to manage and encourage it will survive and those who can't or won't will not. The machine is not physical but social. The Darwinian theory of change and renewal, or extinction as the alternative, is as true of corporate life as of biological life. The constant change in the names and rankings of the companies in Forbes 500 is a contemporary scoreboard of those companies that adapt to a new world and those that do not.

Large companies often build expanding bureaucracies which, like all bureaucracies, need to grow to protect the bureaucrat's turf. Eventually most bureaucracies come to view new ideas and products with alarm. It has been said that the first priority of every bureaucracy becomes the protection of its own members. The layers of management, and the growing length of memos answering other memos, and the decline of face-to-face conversation, all work to curb innovation. And without innovation, companies die over time. One of the central tasks of management, therefore, is to overcome or thin out the underbrush, and to keep alive and well the spirit of entrepreneurship. This spirit can invade both products and marketing. Many successful products were invented before there was any demand for them. The parachute, for example, appeared about three hundred years before the airplane.

Among the discoveries that no one anticipated needing until they suddenly arrived were X-rays, radio and television, photography, sound recording, Einstein's relativity theory, transistors, lasers . . . the list is almost endless. The telephone was not something the public clamored for at the time. In 1879, Sir William Preece, the chief engineer of the British Post Office, testified in the House of Commons that the telephone had little future in Britain. "There are conditions in America which necessitate the use of such instruments more than here," he said. "Here, we have a superabundance of messengers. The absence of servants has compelled Americans to adopt communications systems."

Looking back, it is clear that these judgments are partly funny and partly tragic, but most companies are still making similar decisions about tomorrow's markets.

It is no accident that of the roughly twenty million new jobs created in the U.S. in the last decade, all but about one million were created in new or small entrepreneurial businesses. The explosion of today's technology and marketing is not entirely unlike the explosion of mechanical devices in the late nineteenth century and will no doubt have just as profound an effect.

Our bookshelves today are piled high with books warning us that the pace of change has become too much for human beings to tolerate, that it is not just risk that people fear but the future itself. We are being overwhelmed, we're told, by new technology. When we see what the computer has done and is doing to the world, and consider that it was invented in 1945, this argument may seem plausible. But go back a hundred years to 1846 and the argument falls apart.

That was the year Brigham Young led the Mormons out of Illinois on the way to Utah—and coincidentally the year that saw the invention of the sewing machine and the steel moldboard plow. Historians have called the period that began then and lasted until the outbreak of World War I the heroic age of invention. From the sewing machine in 1846 to the radio vacuum tube in 1911, a major new invention appeared on the average of every fifteen to eighteen months, and was followed almost immediately by a new industry based on the invention. That's what the last half of the nineteenth century was like, but there were not many voices then crying, Stop the world—I want to get off.

There were a few, of course. Not long after Lee De Forest invented the vacuum tube amplifier, he was arrested for stock fraud. He'd been going around saying that his invention would be able to transmit the human voice across the Atlantic. At his trial, the prosecuting attorney declared: "Based on his absurd and deliberately misleading statement, the public, your Honor, has been persuaded to purchase stock in his company."

The jury acquitted De Forest, but the judge admonished him to forget his crackpot inventions and go "get a common, garden-type job and stick to it."

You cannot save something that has not been born, and the saviors are rarely equipped to be the mothers or fathers. The model for perpetual motion is the marriage of management with entrepreneurship. This requires the willingness to listen, to take risks, to realize that some new products or services are customer driven, and some are supply driven. Aluminum, for example, was supply driven. Aluminum pots and pans were not produced in large volume until almost fifty years after the invention, and more decades passed before the airframe manufacturers would call on aluminum-makers to supply many parts. It was, for years, a substance looking for a market. On the other hand, when the world began running out of silkworms, DuPont quickly invented nylon to keep women supplied with stockings.

Then there are some things invented for one purpose that end up doing something else. The phonograph is a case in point. When the telephone was invented, voices could not be transmitted very far, so the idea of a repeating station presented itself. Thomas Edison invented the phonograph as a repeating station. He believed that very few people would be able to afford a telephone and that their messages could be recorded in a central place where one could come and hear them as one would go to a post office to collect mail. He also believed that the most profitable use of the phonograph would be by lawyers recording their clients' last wills and testaments. For this, and doubtless other reasons, it took almost fifteen years to recognize that the phonograph might have a potential for home entertainment.

In what he later admitted to be his greatest mistake, Edison also opposed the use of alternating current—possibly because he already had a large investment in the direct current generators that he had invented. Even Homer sometimes nods.

On a more mundane plane, a whole business was conceived by a man watching college students throwing pie tins to each other instead of returning them to Frisbee Pie Company in Bridgeport. This man, Morrison, took the idea to the Wham-O Company, which made and marketed them by the millions. The Frisbee Pie Company is no more, but the Wham-O product lives on. It's not exactly a high-tech piece of hardware—some may not judge it to be socially useful—but it has created jobs and profits for those who saw its commercial prospects.

When we think about how to measure growth and momentum, we have to acknowledge that some markets are oversupplied—like steel, which is now being produced by eighty-five countries—and some markets are just emerging, like that for one-megabit silicon chips. Some countries try to preserve industries when there is gross overcapacity and some let the market work as new jobs take the place of old. How, then, do we stay in the survivors' column? In my view, we do it by creating a climate in which innovation can grow, and that means planning for the longer-term change, applauding change, not fighting it.

When we perceived, some years ago, that if consumers were paid a fair return on their savings there was no way a brick-and-mortar branch network could earn any money for bank stockholders, we invested heavily in technology for our Citicard machines. We were told by experts in other financial institutions, by financial analysts, and, of course, by the media that (*a*) older people would not use them, (*b*) younger people would not use them, (*c*) men would not use them, and (*d*) women would not use them. As it turned out, none of the above was true, and Citibank alone now handles seventy million transactions a year over its electronic network. We created a customer and built a profitable consumer business when others were getting out of the market.

Most good ideas come from customers who want something new, or want what you sell packaged in a better way, or want it faster at a cheaper price. But there also things the customer does not know he wants, like Frisbees or X-rays, which have to come from the innovators.

Let's go back a moment to Economics 101. We were taught in those days that there are various ways to earn a living. Work, and you get wages. Own some real estate, and you get rent. Have some money, and you can deposit it with your friendly neighborhood banker and collect interest. Notice that we have not mentioned profit.

If wages come from work, rent from real estate, and interest from savings—where do profits come from? The answer is that profits come from risk. The essential difference between the bureaucrat and the entrepreneur is the willingness to take risks. But without the risk-takers, the bureaucrats will ultimately have nothing to administer or regulate.

Obviously, there are unacceptable risks. But the fact that risk is a four-letter word does not mean that we should ban it from our vocabulary. It is the engine that makes the perpetual-motion machine work.

The great economist Joseph Schumpeter addressed this

problem back in 1942. He imagined a world in which Henry Ellsworth, the patent commissioner of 1844, finally turned out to be right. We arrived at "that period when further improvement must end" or when "everything that can be invented has been invented." Here's what Schumpeter predicted:

> A more or less stationary state would ensue. Capitalism, being essentially an evolutionary process, would become atrophic. There would be nothing left for entrepreneurs to do. They would find themselves in much the same situation as generals would in a society perfectly sure of permanent peace. . . . The management of industry and trade would become a matter of current administration, and the personnel would unavoidably acquire the characteristics of a bureaucracy.

The people who insist on seeing only the failures have still another debilitating effect on our society: they frequently manage to make us feel guilty even about our successes.

Malaria, for thousands of years the number one killer of human beings, was finally brought under control after World War II by DDT. But instead of hearing about the tens of millions of human lives that have been saved over the past forty years, we are told about the damage to our natural environment. Concern for the environment is obviously justified, but the highly publicized demonstrations, complete with rock stars and movie actresses, would have us believe that man, and particularly his technology, is single-handedly polluting what would otherwise be a pure and benign nature, something like Disneyland on a nice day in September. Michael Novak has reminded us that this just is not so. He writes:

> Nature was raw and cruel to nature long before human beings intervened. It may be doubted whether human beings have ever done one-tenth of the polluting to nature that nature has done to itself. There is infinitely more methane gas—poisonous in one respect and damaging to the environment—generated by the

swamps of Florida and other parts of the United States than by all the automobile pollution of all the places on this planet. In our superhuman efforts to be nice and feel guilty, we sometimes try to take all the credit for pollution improperly.

Be nice, feel guilty, and play safe. If there was ever a prescription for producing a dismal future, that has to be it. It is a sure prescription for the demise of our way of life.

It is almost impossible to exaggerate the importance to the general welfare of the willingness of individuals to take a personal risk. The worst thing that can happen to a society, as to an individual, is to become terrified of uncertainty. Uncertainty is an invitation to innovate, to create; uncertainty is the blank page in the author's typewriter, the granite block before a sculptor, the capital in the hands of an investor, or the problem challenging the inventive mind of a scientist or an engineer. In short, uncertainty is the opportunity to make the world a better place.

Despite this, everything in our national life today seems designed to encourage our natural caution. The tax structure discourages the innovators, penalizes the successful, and preserves the inefficient. Even many medicines in common use around the world to prevent human suffering are denied to Americans on the slender grounds that an overdosed mouse has contracted a tumor. This is not prudence. Prudence is one of the intellectual virtues, and there is very little intelligence to be found in all this. It is institutionalized timidity, and I submit that it does not represent the will of the vast majority of the American people.

If we observe the world around us, Americans as individuals seek out risk. Every child who plays football, or hockey, or any other contact sport, risks injury. There is no shortage of test pilots for new aircraft, nor of candidates for any of the other hazardous jobs in our society, including the job of President of the United States. If we perceive that life is too easy, we put sand traps and other obstacles on the golf course and create artificial hazards where none exist. In short, risk is a necessary part of life and one that belongs on our list of natural rights.

Let those who seek a perpetual safe harbor continue to do so. Let them renounce risk for themselves, if they choose. What no one has a right to do is renounce it for all the rest of us, or to pursue the chimerical goal of a risk-free society for some by eliminating the rewards of risk for everyone.

The society that promises no risks, and whose leaders use the word "risk" only as a pejorative, may be able to protect life, but there will be no liberty, and very little pursuit of happiness. You will look in vain in the Federalist Papers, the Declaration of Independence, or the Constitution for promises of a safe, easy, risk-free life. Indeed, when Woodrow Wilson called for a world safe for democracy, it was left to Gilbert Chesterton to put that sentiment in perspective. "Impossible," he said. "Democracy is a dangerous trade."

Index

■

27 million Americans can't read a bedtime story to a child.

It's because 27 million adults in this country simply can't read.

Functional illiteracy has reached one out of five Americans. It robs them of even the simplest of human pleasures, like reading a fairy tale to a child.

You can change all this by joining the fight against illiteracy.

Call the Coalition for Literacy at toll-free **1-800-228-8813** and volunteer.

**Volunteer
Against Illiteracy.
The only degree you need
is a degree of caring.**

Ad Council Coalition for Literacy